LORD KITCHENER AND
WINSTON CHURCHILL: THE DARDANELLES
PART I, 1914–15

uncovered editions

Series editor: Tim Coates

Other titles in the series

uncovered editions

LORD KITCHENER AND WINSTON CHURCHILL

THE DARDANELLES COMMISSION PART I, 1914–15

∞⋘⋙∞

London: The Stationery Office

© The Stationery Office 2000

Applications for reproduction should be made in writing to
The Stationery Office Limited, St Crispins, Duke Street,
Norwich NR3 1PD.

ISBN 0 11 702423 6

First published as Cd 8490, 1917
© Crown copyright

A CIP catalogue record for this book is available from the
British Library.

Cover photograph © The British Library. Photographer:
George Barrow, China 1900-1901.

Typeset by J&L Composition Ltd, Filey, North Yorkshire.

Printed in the United Kingdom for The Stationery Office by
Biddles Ltd, Guildford, Surrey.

TJ2744   C10   10/00

Uncovered Editions are historic official papers which have not previously been available in a popular form. The series has been created directly from the archive of The Stationery Office in London, and the books have been chosen for the quality of their story-telling. Some subjects are familiar, but others are less well known. Each is a moment of history.

❧❦❧

Series editor: Tim Coates

Tim Coates studied at University College, Oxford and at the University of Stirling. After working in the theatre for a number of years, he took up bookselling and became managing director, firstly of Sherratt and Hughes bookshops, and then of Waterstone's. He is known for his support for foreign literature, particularly from the Czech Republic. The idea for "Uncovered Editions" came while searching through the bookshelves of his late father-in-law, Air Commodore Patrick Cave OBE. He is married to Bridget Cave, has two sons, and lives in London.

This is the first report to Parliament of the commission set up to review the Dardanelles campaign in which the British, with their Allies, invaded the Gallipoli Peninsula during World War I (1914–18). It was published in early 1917.

The second report will be published in this series with the title "Defeat at Gallipoli: The Dardanelles Commission Part II, 1915–16".

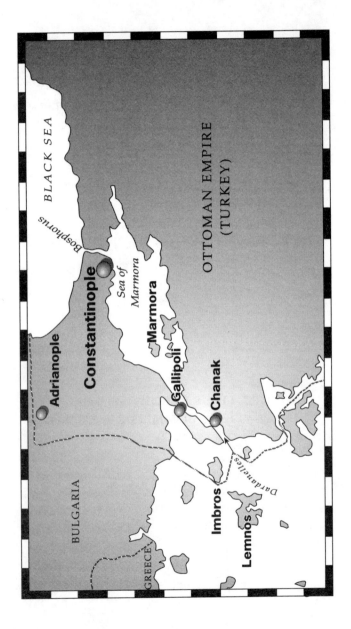

∘⚬⚭✕⚮⚬∘

THE FIRST REPORT OF THE DARDANELLES COMMISSION (Cd. 8490, 1917)

Extracted from the inquiry into the origin, inception and conduct of operations of war in the Dardanelles and Gallipoli from 4th August 1914 (outbreak of war with Germany) to 23rd March 1915 (when idea of naval attack was abandoned).

List of witnesses examined

Date [*of examination in 1916*]		Name	Functions in the Autumn of 1914 and the Spring of 1915
September	19th	Lieut.-Col. Sir Maurice Hankey, K.C.B.	Secretary to the War Council.
,,	27th	Do.	
,,	26th	Viscount Grey of Fallodon, K.G.	Secretary of State for Foreign Affairs.
,,	28th	The Rt. Hon. W. S. Churchill	First Lord of the Admiralty.
October	4th	Do.	
,,	24th	Do.	
,,	25th	Do.	
,,	26th	Do.	
,,	5th	Commodore de Bartolomé, C.B.	Naval Secretary to the First Lord of the Admiralty.
,,	5th	Vice-Admiral Sir Henry Oliver, K.C.B., M.V.O.	Chief of the War Staff.
,,	25th	Do.	
,,	5th	Admiral of the Fleet Sir Arthur Wilson, G.C.B., O.M., V.C., G.C.V.O.	Member of the War Staff Group at the Admiralty.
,,	6th	Admiral Sir Henry Jackson, K.C.B., K.C.V.O., F.R.S.	Admiralty Staff.
,,	6th	Vice-Admiral Sir Sackville Carden, K.C.M.G.	In command of the Mediterranean Fleet up to March 17th.

List of witnesses examined—continued

Date [of examination in 1916]		Name	Functions in the Autumn of 1914 and the Spring of 1915
October	10th	Lieut.-General Sir James Wolfe Murray, K.C.B.	Chief of the Imperial General Staff.
,,	10th	Vice-Admiral Sir John de Robeck, K.C.B.	In command of the Mediterranean Fleet from March 17th.
,,	10th	Rear-Admiral F. Tudor, C.B.	Third Sea Lord of the Admiralty.
,,	10th	Commodore Cecil Lambert	Fourth Sea Lord of the Admiralty.
,,	13th	Do.	
,,	10th	Sir Graham Greene, K.C.B.	Secretary to the Admiralty.
,,	24th	Do.	
,,	11th	Admiral of the Fleet Lord Fisher of Kilverstone, G.C.B., O.M., G.C.V.O.	First Sea Lord of the Admiralty.
,,	12th	Major-General H. Hickman	Commanding the Plymouth Garrison.
,,	12th	Major-General Charles Callwell, C.B.	Director of Military Operations.
,,	12th	Brigadier-General Sir George Aston, K.C.B.	Employed at the Admiralty up to the end of August, 1914.
,,	12th	Admiral Sir F. Hamilton, K.C.B., C.V.O.	Second Sea Lord of the Admiralty.

List of witnesses examined—*continued*

Date [*of examination in 1916*]		Name	Functions in the Autumn of 1914 and the Spring of 1915
October	12th	Rear-Admiral Morgan Singer, C.B.	Director of Naval Ordnance at the Admiralty.
,,	12th	Sir Reginald Brade, K.C.B.	Permanent Under-Secretary at the War Office.
,,	13th	The Rt. Hon. A.J. Balfour, P.C.	Generally summoned to the War Council.
,,	13th	General Sir Ian Hamilton, K.C.B., D.S.O.	In command at the Dardanelles from March 13th (date of leaving London).
,,	18th	Rear-Admiral Thomas Jackson, C.B., M.V.O.	Director of the Operations Division of the Admiralty War Staff.
,,	18th	Viscount Haldane of Cloan, K.T.	Lord Chancellor.
,,	18th	Field-Marshal Viscount French, O.M., K.C.M.G., & c.	Commanding the Expeditionary Force in France.
,,	24th	Captain Hall, R.N.	Director of the Intelligence Division of the Admiralty.
,,	24th	Vice-Admiral Sir Reginald Bacon, K.C.B., D.S.O.	Now in command of the Dover Patrol.

List of witnesses examined—continued

Date [*of examination in 1916*]		Name	Functions in the Autumn of 1914 and the Spring of 1915
October	26th	The Marquis of Crewe, K.G., P. C.	Secretary of State for India.
,,	30th	The Rt. Hon. D. Lloyd George, P. C.	Chancellor of the Exchequer.
,,	31st	Commander Hubbard	Retired Royal Naval Reserve. Formerly in the Turkish Service.
,,	31st	The Rt. Hon. H. Asquith, P. C.	Prime Minister.
November	8th	The Rt. Hon. R. McKenna, P. C.	Secretary of State for the Home Department.
December	1st	Sir George Arthur, Bart.	Private Secretary to Lord Kitchener.
,,	4th	Major-General Sir Stanley Von Donop, K.C.B.	Master-General of the Ordnance.
,,	4th	H.J. Creedy, Esq., C.B.	Private Secretary to Lord Kitchener.

Note: It will be observed that, with the exception of Commander Hubbard, who, after retiring from the Royal Naval Reserve, was employed as a captain in the Turkish Navy, all the witnesses who have appeared before us occupy, or have occupied, official positions. It is, indeed, obvious that none but officials could throw any light upon the special subject which has, up to the present time, engaged our attention.

The Dardanelles

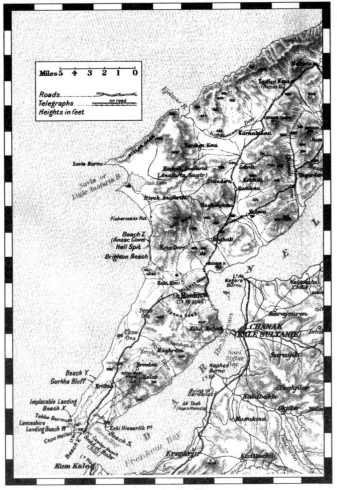

◦◦◊◊◊◦◦

Introductory notes

In the first place, it has to be remembered that the events which we shall have to narrate happened in the last five months of 1914 or the first three months of 1915; that at that time a very heavy strain of work was thrown on all the Departments of the Government which were concerned; that in respect to many points of considerable importance the various witnesses called have had, in the absence of complete written records, to speak from memory of what actually

occurred, and that the constant strain of work result-
ing from subsequent events of equal, or perhaps even
of greater, importance may possibly, in view of the
period which has elapsed, have, to some extent,
obscured their recollection of all the circumstances. It
can, therefore, be no matter for surprise that the evidence given as to the views expressed at the time by
some of the leading officials should be, in certain
cases, somewhat conflicting.

We have, of course, attached special importance
to opinions which were unquestionably expressed
during the period when the desirability or otherwise
of making an attack on the Dardanelles was under
consideration. Without casting any sort of imputation
on the good faith of the witnesses themselves, it is
conceivable that, in giving to the Commission an
account of the past they may have been to some
extent unconsciously influenced by their knowledge
of subsequent events.

In the second place, we have to remark that the
premature and deeply regretted death of Lord
Kitchener naturally renders it impossible for us to
state, with the same confidence as that which obtains
in the case of living witnesses, whether we have faith-
fully represented the opinions he entertained and the
aims which he had in view at different periods of the
proceedings. The difficulty is enhanced owing to the
strong opinion which Lord Kitchener entertained as
to the absolute necessity of maintaining the strictest
secrecy in respect to all matters connected with military operations. Sir Maurice Hankey, indeed, stated

that some difficulties at times arose owing to Lord Kitchener's unwillingness to impart full information even to the members of the War Council. We have, however, done all that is possible to ascertain both his views and intentions by closely examining such contemporaneous records as exist and by enquiry from those who were associated with him during his lifetime. It is, in this connection, singularly unfortunate that that gallant officer, Colonel Fitzgerald, who was Lord Kitchener's personal military secretary, and who was probably better acquainted with his opinions than any other individual, shared the fate of his distinguished chief.

We have not thought that we should be justified, in deference to the consideration which is rightly shown to the memory of the illustrious dead, in abstaining from a complete revelation of the action which Lord Kitchener took during the various phases of the events under consideration, nor have we hesitated to express our views on that action. It is necessary to do justice to the living as well as to the dead.

Moreover, it must be steadfastly borne in mind that, at the time when the attack on the Dardanelles was under consideration, Lord Kitchener occupied a position such as has probably never been held by any previous Secretary of State for War. The circumstances of the case cannot be understood unless the nature of his position is fully realised. In this connection, we may quote the following passage from the evidence given by Mr. Winston Churchill: "Lord Kitchener's personal qualities and position played at this time a very great part in the decision of events. His prestige and authority were immense. He was the sole mouthpiece of War Office opinion in the War Council. Everyone had the greatest admiration for his character, and everyone felt fortified, amid the terrible and incalculable events of the opening months of the war, by his commanding presence. When he gave a decision it was invariably accepted as final. He was never, to my belief, overruled by the War Council or the Cabinet in any military matter, great or small. No single unit was ever sent or withheld contrary, not merely to his agreement, but to his advice. Scarcely anyone ever ventured to argue with him in Council. Respect for the man, sympathy for him in his immense labours, confidence in his professional judgment, and the belief that he had plans deeper and wider than any we could see, silenced misgivings and disputes, whether in the Council or at the War Office. All-powerful, imperturbable, reserved, he dominated absolutely our counsels at this time. If the course of my observations and the documents it is my duty to lay before you appear to constitute any reflection upon his military policy, I wish here to testify to the overwhelming weight of the burdens laid upon him, to his extraordinary courage and patience in all the difficulties and perplexities through which we were passing and to his unvarying kindness to me."

Although, however, we have thought that we should be failing in our duty if we did not deal fully with the part Lord Kitchener played in these transactions, we would ask those who may read this report to remember, in justice to his memory, in the first place, that it has not been possible to check his recorded opinions by the light of subsequent explanation, and, secondly, that if, in the eyes of any critics, he may, under circumstances of very great difficulty, be held to have committed some errors of judgment, the fact cannot in any way obscure the very distinguished services which he rendered to his country in other directions.

The Committee of Imperial Defence

Before proceeding to deal with the facts connected
with the origin and inception of the Dardanelles
Expedition, we think it will be desirable to explain, in
the first place, the higher organisation for the conduct
of war which prevailed at the time of its outbreak,
and, secondly, the changes which were subsequently
made in that organisation. Further, we trust that we
are not interpreting erroneously the wishes either of

His Majesty's Government or of the Legislature when we say that, if our enquiry is to be of any real practical use for future guidance, we should not confine ourselves to a bald statement of facts, or even to the mere assignment of a proper share of responsibility to individuals or departments in connection with past events, but that we should go somewhat further and indicate briefly and in general terms the conclusions at which we have arrived in respect to the merits and demerits of the original, as also of the revised organisations which have been instrumental in conducting the war. It would, however, be exceeding the scope of our functions if we were to discuss in detail the measures which should be taken to remedy any administrative defects which the light of recent experience has revealed.

Before the war, and after its outbreak until nearly the end of November, 1914, the higher direction of military and naval operations was vested in the Cabinet, who were assisted by the Committee of Imperial Defence. This Committee was tentatively initiated in 1901 and reconstructed in 1904. The main functions of the Secretariat, as set forth in a Treasury Minute dated May 4th of that year, were "to collect and co-ordinate for the use of the Committee information bearing on the wide problem of Imperial Defence," and "to make possible a continuity of method in the treatment of the questions which may from time to time come before the Committee." It was laid down that the Committee was to be "merely a consultative or advisory body." This view was frequently confirmed in statements made by responsible Ministers in Parliament. It is quite correct in this sense that the Committee exercised no executive functions, that it was not a body which supervised the proceedings of the War Office or the Admiralty, that it was not a Court of Appeal against the decisions of either of those two Departments, and that it did not interfere in any War Office or Admiralty details. Nevertheless, the view that the Committee was purely advisory requires some qualification.

In practice, it did more than advise. It decided. On being asked whether the Committee "decided on certain courses," the Secretary, Sir Maurice Hankey, replied in the affirmative, and, on being further asked whether "action was taken on their decisions," he replied: "Yes, what would happen would be that after the meeting the conclusion would be notified by me officially to the Department responsible for taking action."

It might, at first sight, perhaps be thought that, under such circumstances, the Committee might possibly encroach on the constitutional prerogatives of the Cabinet. Fears that this would happen have, indeed, from time to time been expressed. In dealing with this subject, however, the composition of the Committee has to be borne in mind. It varied slightly as occasion might demand, but the Prime Minister was always the President, and he usually invited the attendance of the Chancellor of the Exchequer, the Secretaries of State for War, Foreign Affairs and India, and also the First Lord of the Admiralty.

Mr. Arthur Balfour, although not at the time of which we are now treating a member of the Cabinet, was also usually invited to attend the meetings both of the Committee of Imperial Defence and of the War Council which subsequently took its place. On the one hand, when any question came before the Cabinet, several of its most important members were, it is true, already pledged to views expressed in their capacities of Members of the Committee of Imperial Defence. On the other hand, the united Cabinet had the great advantage of learning the opinions which their colleagues had formed on any particular subject after it had been discussed in the presence of qualified experts. The Committee of Imperial Defence was, in fact, for all practical purposes, a Committee of the Cabinet with some experts added. It does not appear that the creation of such a body in any way fails to harmonise with sound constitutional practice.

Before leaving this branch of the subject, it may be remarked that, in explaining the functions of the Committee of Imperial Defence, Sir Maurice Hankey said that they had been "laid down in time of peace, and with a view to peace requirements." The natural result ensued. Very shortly after the outbreak of war, the Committee, although never formally abolished, fell into abeyance. Another institution was substituted in its place. It appears to us that a body such as the Committee of Imperial Defence, whose sole duty it is to prepare for war, should be organised to meet the requirements not of peace, but of war. We should add that the reason which dictated the transformation of the Committee of Imperial Defence was based, not so much on any defect inherent in that institution itself, but rather on the proved necessity of curtailing the number of members of the Cabinet who actually participated in the conduct of the war.

∞⟡∞

The War Council

From the commencement of the war until November
25th, 1914—that is to say, for a period of nearly four
months—no change was made in the machinery for
the superior conduct of naval and military operations.
That machinery consisted, as we have already mentioned, of the Cabinet, assisted by the Committee of
Imperial Defence, with the War Office and the
Admiralty acting as its executive agents. The Cabinet
at that time consisted of twenty-two members. It

must have been obvious from the first that it was far too numerous to control effectively the conduct of the war, more especially by reason of the fact that many of the Ministers presided over Departments which, in some cases, were very slightly and, in others, were in no degree concerned with warlike operations.

It is to be regretted that this rudimentary fact was not recognised immediately after the outbreak of war. Thus, for four months, during which time events of the utmost importance were occurring, the machinery employed for designing and controlling the higher operations of the war was both clumsy and inefficient. Eventually some improvement was effected. The War Council took the place of the Committee of Imperial Defence.

The composition and functions of the War Council did not materially differ from those of the Committee of Imperial Defence. A change of some importance was, however, made in the procedure. It had been the practice to pass round the notes of the proceedings at the meetings of the Committee of Imperial Defence to all the members who had been present, and who were thus able to correct any inaccuracies that might occur in the representation of their views. Owing to the great press of business, this practice was abandoned by the War Council. Longhand notes were, indeed, kept by the Secretary, but these, of course, cannot carry the same authority as corrected minutes.

A very full and, we believe, accurate account of

what occurred in connection with the Dardanelles Expedition at the various meetings of the Council was, however, furnished to us by the Secretary, and the full text of the notes, which record the proceedings in many matters wholly unconnected with the Dardanelles Expedition, was placed at the disposal of our Chairman, who was able to assure us of the general adequacy and correctness of the summary communicated to us by Sir Maurice Hankey.

The main change which was effected was, however, in connection with the powers of the Council as compared to those of the Committee of Imperial Defence. Whilst the latter body was in existence, the responsibility for all important decisions remained, theoretically in all, and practically in most cases, with the united Cabinet. The War Council remained, like the Committee of Imperial Defence, a Committee of the Cabinet with some experts added. Theoretically, the powers of the united Cabinet remained the same as before. Practically, they underwent a radical change.

It was the Council, and not the united Cabinet, which finally decided the most important matters, and gave effect to its decisions without necessarily waiting for any expression of assent or dissent from the Cabinet. The Cabinet appear to have been generally informed of any important decisions which may have been taken by the Council, but not until after the necessary executive steps had been taken to give whole or partial effect to those decisions. This is what actually happened in the case both of the naval and military operations undertaken at the Dardanelles.

Further, we have been given to understand that some members of the Cabinet did not wish to be informed of what was going on. Mr. Winston Churchill, in the course of his examination, said: "I have often heard the Cabinet say: 'We do not wish to be told about this—this is a secret matter, and the fewer who know about it the better.'"

It would be an exaggeration to say that, in consequence of this method of conducting business, those members of the Cabinet who did not attend the meetings of the War Council were relieved of all responsibility in connection with the conduct of the war. But their responsibility was slight. It was limited to the fact that they, very rightly in our opinion, were content to delegate the full powers of the united Cabinet to their colleagues who were members of the War Council.

For all practical purposes it may be held that, during the period under review, the powers and prerogatives of the united Cabinet were, in so far as the conduct of the war was concerned, held almost entirely in abeyance. The correctness of this view is confirmed by the testimony of Mr. McKenna, who, although a member of the Cabinet, did not, during the early stages of the war, attend the meetings of the War Council. Mr. McKenna was asked the following question by the Chairman:—

"Should I be correct in stating broadly that the responsibility of the united Cabinet amounted to this, that they had delegated their powers more or less to the War Council?"

His reply was: "If I may say so, I think you have expressed it absolutely. There was a general acceptance by the Cabinet of the constitution and action of the War Council. But if the question is put to me that the Cabinet had in any real sense any responsibility for the individual decisions of the War Council, whether communicated to them or not, I can only say that, for my own part, it would be asking the Cabinet to accept the responsibility without any means of judging."

Further, a distinction has to be made between the real responsibility which devolved on the several Cabinet Ministers who were members of the War Council. The Chancellor of the Exchequer (Mr. Lloyd George), the Secretary of State for Foreign Affairs (Sir Edward, now Viscount Grey of Fallodon) and the Secretary of State for India (the Marquis of Crewe) exercised undoubted and very legitimate influence, and occasionally stated their opinions, but the main responsibility rested on three members of the Council—namely, the Prime Minister (Mr. Asquith), the Secretary of State for War (Lord Kitchener) and the First Lord of the Admiralty (Mr. Winston Churchill).

The latter, in the course of his evidence, said: "In the early stages the war was carried on by the Prime Minister, and Lord Kitchener and me, I think, in the next place, but I was on a rather different plane. I had not the same weight or authority as those two Ministers, nor the same power, and if they said, This is to be done or not to be done, that settled it."

We believe this description of the actual working of the machine to be substantially correct, save that Mr. Winston Churchill probably assigned to himself a more unobtrusive part than that which he actually played.

It is obvious that the main questions which came under the consideration of the War Council in connection with the Dardanelles operations were of a highly technical nature on which the opinions only of those who were possessed of naval or military knowledge or experience would be of any real value. It is, therefore, essential to ascertain, with as great a degree of accuracy as possible, what was the precise position assigned to the expert members of the Council. We have devoted much attention to this subject. We think that the best plan which can be adopted in order to explain the situation will be to quote passages from the evidence both of the experts themselves and of the Ministers who were members of the Council.

It is clear that, in dealing with this question, a distinction has to be drawn between the War Office and the Admiralty.

The Secretary of State for War (Lord Kitchener) was himself a distinguished expert. The only other officer possessing military experience who regularly attended the meetings of the Council was Lieutenant-General Sir James Wolfe Murray, who, on October 25th, 1914, succeeded the late Sir Charles Douglas as Chief of the Imperial General Staff. Sir James Murray told us that "Lord Kitchener acted very much as his own Chief of the Staff." When asked whether he "considered himself the

Staff Officer of Lord Kitchener and that he was not called upon to express any independent opinion unless he was especially asked to do so," he replied, "Certainly." He added that he was "never asked" to express any opinion.

The case of the Admiralty was different. The First Lord (Mr. Winston Churchill) was not himself an expert. Expert naval advice was represented by Lord Fisher, the First Sea Lord, and by Sir Arthur Wilson, who, although he did not occupy any official position at the Admiralty, was, from the commencement of the war, habitually consulted both by the First Lord and the First Sea Lord. On one important occasion (January 28th) Sir Henry Oliver was also present.

The view taken by Lord Fisher of his own position at the War Council may be gathered from the following extract from his evidence:—

> "*The Chairman.* I should like you to explain why you thought that at the War Council there were only two alternatives before you, one to yield your opinion absolutely and the other to resign. You were a consultative body. Is it possible to carry on business with a consultative body on such a basis as that?
>
> *A.* I can make it clear to you. The War Council only consisted of the Cabinet Ministers. We were not members of the War Council. I was not a member of the War Council, nor was Sir Arthur Wilson, nor Sir James Wolfe Murray. It is a mistake to call us members of the War Council—it was no such thing. We were the experts there who were to open our mouths when told to.

Q. Nothing else?

A. Nothing else.

Q. And you did not consider yourselves members of the War Council?

A. Absolutely not. The members of the Cabinet were members of the Council, and the others were simply there ready to answer questions if asked.

Q. And they never were asked?

A. They were sometimes, because I was asked how many battleships would be lost, and I said twelve.

Q. But they were never asked anything about the Dardanelles?

A. No."

The following extract from Sir Arthur Wilson's evidence shows that the view which he took of his position was generally identical with that entertained by Lord Fisher.

"*The Chairman*. I want to understand what exactly your position, and that of the other members of the Council, was, because when the First Lord expounded the naval view if you did not agree would it not have been your duty to say so?

A. Probably not, unless I was asked. I was there to help the First Lord.

Q. And you were never asked?

A. No.

Q. And you were there to help the First Lord?

A. Yes.

Q. But not necessarily to agree with him?

A. Not to express agreement if I did not agree, but not to oppose him when it was not a matter which specially concerned me."

It is now necessary to explain the light in which the Ministerial Members of the Council regarded the position occupied by the experts.

Mr. Winston Churchill stated: "Whenever I went to the War Council I always insisted on being accompanied by the First Sea Lord and Sir Arthur Wilson, and when, at the War Council, I spoke in the name of the Admiralty, I was not expressing simply my own views, but I was expressing to the best of my ability the opinions we had agreed upon at our daily group meetings; and I was expressing these opinions in the presence of two naval colleagues and friends who had the right, the knowledge, and the power at any moment to correct me or dissent from what I said, and who were fully cognisant of their rights."

Viscount Grey of Fallodon said that the War Council "went entirely in these naval and military matters by the opinions expressed by the two Ministers." Further, he was asked the following question by Sir William Pickford:—

"I think we were told that of course the First Lord of the Admiralty would put the view of the Admiralty, and if the First Sea Lord were present and said nothing he would be taken to assent to the plan?"

To this he replied: "I think the natural assumption would be that either he actively assented, or that he did not think it of sufficient importance to record a separate opinion, or did not desire to record a separate opinion, whatever the reason might be."

Mr. Arthur Balfour's views may be gathered from the following extracts from his evidence:—

"*The Chairman.* We want to arrive particularly at what was your view and the views of others similarly placed to yourself on the position of the expert advisers towards the War Council?

A. I think they were there to offer technical professional advice upon questions on which they could speak with authority, but on which a layman could not speak with authority.

Q. Do you think they were under any obligation to initiate opinions or merely to wait until they were asked?

A. That would depend on the view the Chairman took of their duties. My own view is that if professional advisers are present at such a Council as that, it is the business of the Chairman, and perhaps of other members, to see that nothing is passed over their heads on which they have an opinion until the opinion has been extracted.

Q. With regard to any decision taken when the expert advisers did not express dissent, would you from that infer that they assented?

A. I should certainly assume that.

Q. And if they dissented they must express dissent at the meeting?

A. I should certainly have assumed that.

Q. Will you refer to Lord Fisher's evidence?

A. Having read that, I do not assent to it as a broad question of principle. I think it is true that a technical adviser brought into a meeting of Cabinet Ministers might not care to start or initiate a discussion, but if the question before the Committee was, Do the Admiralty or do the War Office concur with such and such a view, with such and such a question, I certainly do not think they ought to be silent if they do not agree.

Q. Supposing the Chief of a Department, taking particularly the Admiralty, presents certain views and gives the Council generally to understand that his expert advisers are behind him and agree to those views, do you think it would be the duty of the expert advisers present to say, 'That does not represent our views'?

A. I think the expert advisers—I do not refer particularly to Lord Fisher or Sir Arthur Wilson, but generally—if they feel their expert advice is not before the Council, that the Council are not aware of what their views are, ought to take means for letting their views be known. It need not necessarily be an interruption of the proceedings, thrusting themselves in, as it were, in the discussion, though that would be the natural method of doing it.

Q. You look to them to state their opinions in the event of any expert advice being given in which they do not agree. Would you make a distinction between expert advice and matters of policy for the Cabinet?

A. Certainly.

Q. We have had evidence given on this point, and Sir Arthur Wilson distinctly says he did not think he was called upon to give any opinion whatever, unless he was asked to do so, and there is a very similar statement by Lord Fisher, who, in fact, goes very far in that direction. I think I am not incorrectly stating both their views when I say they stated that they were there to be what they called loyal to their Chief, and in fact they were not to contradict him, and Lord Fisher goes so far as to say, when I pointed out to him that it was very difficult to carry on any consultation on that basis, that the only alternative left for him was to hold his tongue, though he dissented, or to resign. Does that suggest itself to you?

A. I dissent personally from that method of conducting business. I do not believe it is any use having in experts unless you try and get at their inner thoughts on the technical questions before the Council.

Q. The military experts stood on rather a different footing, because during the period we are discussing Lord Kitchener was himself a military expert. We have had Sir James Wolfe Murray here, and he said that both in respect to his position at the War Office and in respect to his position on the Council he considered himself in the light of Lord Kitchener's Staff Officer and nothing else?

A. That may be so, and I think you are right in saying that Lord Kitchener's position was exceptional: though even there personally I think it is very little use having an expert present except to remind his Chief of particular facts and give him particular statistics, unless you are to find out what his opinion is.

Q. But, of course, there was a great difference in Lord Kitchener's position and Mr. Churchill's position, because Lord Kitchener was himself an expert and a distinguished soldier, whereas Mr. Churchill had to rely on others. You think, then, it was the duty of the naval experts there to dissent if anything was said which did not represent their views?

A. Yes, with this qualification. I think their task ought to be facilitated by the Cabinet Ministers present, the Heads of their Departments or the Cabinet Minister who was in the chair.

Q. By asking them?

A. By asking them."

Viscount Haldane of Cloan, who was at the time Lord Chancellor, gave the following evidence:—

"*The Chairman*. Did you generally hold the view that if they (the expert members) did not dissent they assented?

A. I thought so, because they were there for the purpose of giving us information ...

Q. You expected Lord Fisher, if he had any great objection, to state it at the Council?

A. I certainly did ... If they (Lord Fisher and Sir Arthur Wilson) were what they were at the Defence Committee; it was their business to give the counsel which they were called there to give, and if they misunderstood their position they ought to have found out what it was. I am perfectly certain that if Lord Fisher had said to the Prime Minister, 'Do you wish me to speak?' he would have said, 'I most certainly do,' and we all did. We all looked upon him as there to take counsel with us.

Q. In fact, you do not concur in the view of the War Council as expressed by Lord Fisher?

A. I do not. I think it is an excusable thing from the fact that the body sat in the Cabinet room in Downing Street instead of 2, Whitehall Gardens, and that there were a good many Cabinet Ministers present. For the rest, I think it was just the old Defence Committee, and certainly they had every opportunity of uttering as much as they liked. Not one of us was asked to speak. Questions were not put round. It was a general question.

Q. And you also relied wholly on what the experts said at the Council, and nothing else? You did not go outside that at all? If they did not express dissent at the Council you considered they more or less assented?

A. Yes. When I heard it said, for instance, 'We have considered it and we think the forts can be reduced within a certain time, and with a certain expenditure of ammunition,' and the details were given to us, and Lord Fisher and Sir Arthur Wilson sat silent, I thought he (the First Lord of the Admiralty) was giving the view of the Admiralty War Staff, of which Lord Fisher was the head."

Lord Crewe, who was at the time Secretary of State for India, expressed the opinion "that the political members of the Committee did too much of the talking and the expert members as a rule too little"— a view in which Lord Haldane also concurred.

Lord Crewe further said that the fact that the expert members did not express dissent at the meetings involved in his opinion, either "assent or at any rate acquiescence." On being asked whether he "expected that they (the experts) would express dissent on technical matters unless their chief represented their views," he replied, "Unquestionably."

Mr. Lloyd George did not concur in the description given by Lord Fisher of the position he occupied on the War Council. On being asked the question, "If the experts present did not express dissent, did you assume that they assented to what was done?" he replied "Certainly."

The views entertained by the Prime Minister on the point now under discussion are, of course, of special importance. Mr. Asquith stated that he did not concur in the view that it was the duty of the experts on the Council only to give their opinions if they were asked. When asked whether he held that if the experts did not dissent from the views expressed by the Heads of their Departments, it would be held that they assented, he replied: "Normally and regularly, yes." Speaking of an important meeting which took place on January 13th, Mr. Asquith said: "I should have expected any of the experts there, if they entertained a strong personal view on their own expert authority, to express it."

Sir Maurice Hankey gave the following evidence:—

"*Lord Nicholson*: You were asked about the procedure of the Committee of Imperial Defence. Is it not the custom, when a naval or military member does not say anything after the First Lord or the Secretary of State speaks, to admit that he concurs, otherwise there would be such a lot of talk?

A. Yes, that is certainly very strongly my view.

Q. And to avoid conversation as much as possible, if you do not object, either the First Lord speaks or the Secretary of State speaks?

A. Yes.

Q. If one or the other remains silent it is understood that he concurs?

A. Yes."

There is one further feature in connection with the methods adopted in conducting the business of the War Council to which it is necessary to draw attention. The evidence as to whether, at the close of each meeting, the decisions were read out and understood by all present is contradictory. Thus, as regards a very important meeting held on January 13th, 1915, to which we shall presently revert, Sir Arthur Wilson, in reply to a question addressed to him, said: "I was under the impression that no decision had been taken at all." The following dialogue then ensued:—

> "*The Chairman.* If you thought there had been a decision taken would you have said you did not agree to it?
>
> *A.* No.
>
> *Q.* Why not?
>
> *A.* Because it was not my business. I was not in any way connected with the question, and it had never in any way officially been put before me."

Sir James Murray, in answer to a question addressed to him by Mr. Clyde, said: "I sometimes left the War Council with a very indistinct idea of any decision having been arrived at at all."

Speaking of the meeting of January 13th, Lord Fisher said:

> "I have not the least doubt a decision was come to, because very likely the Prime Minister went and wrote it down when the meeting was over, but it was never read out to us that that was the decision.
>
> *Q.* You were not aware that any decision was come to?
>
> *A.* No; I do not remember it; no more does Wilson."

On the other hand, Mr. Asquith states very positively that the decision taken on January 13th was read out before the Council broke up, although possibly some of the members may have left before this was done. Mr. Asquith's description of what occurred is confirmed by Sir Maurice Hankey.

The following are the conclusions to be drawn from the evidence which we have received as to the proceedings of the War Council:—

1. It was not the practice to ask the experts attending the Council to express their opinions.

2. The experts themselves did not consider it their duty either to express any opinions unless they were asked to do so, or to intimate dissent, at the Council board, if they disagreed with the views set forth by the Ministers in charge of their respective Departments.

3. The Chairman and the Ministerial members of the War Council looked to the naval and military experts to express their opinions if they dissented from the views put forward by the heads of their respective departments. As the experts did not express their opinions the Council was in technical matters guided wholly by the views laid before them by the Secretary of State for War and the First Lord of the Admiralty.

4. The functions of the experts were, to a great extent, differently understood by the experts themselves and the Ministerial members of the Council.

We have dwelt at some length on this subject, as it has a very important bearing on the events which we are about to narrate.

⚬◦◦ΩΩ◦◦⚬

The Admiralty

The Committee of Imperial Defence was not the
only body which underwent considerable changes
after the outbreak of the war. Important alterations
were also made in the methods of conducting business both at the Admiralty and the War Office.

The authority of the Board of Admiralty is based
on Letters Patent issued under the Great Seal in pur-
suance of certain Acts of Parliament, and on various
Orders in Council, the latest and most important of

which bear the dates of August 10th, 1904, January 7th, 1912, and July 19th, 1912.

The Board consisted at the commencement of the war, and still consists, of:—

A First Lord.
Four Sea Lords.
Two Civil Lords.
The Parliamentary Secretary.
The Permanent Secretary.

The First Lord is "solely responsible to the Crown and Parliament for all the business of the Admiralty."

The functions of the First Sea Lord are defined, *inter alia*, in the following terms:—

"Preparation for war. All large questions of Naval policy and Maritime warfare—to advise."

The other members of the Board are charged with various Departmental duties.

Neither the First Lord, nor the First Sea Lord, are under any legal obligation to consult either the Board collectively or any individual members of the Board, but the "Official Procedure and Rules," p. 51, contains the following note:—

"It is to be understood that in any matter of great importance the First Sea Lord is always to be consulted by the other Sea Lords, the Civil Lord, the Additional Civil Lord, and the Parliamentary and Permanent Secretaries; but each Member of the Board and the Parliamentary and Permanent Secretaries will communicate direct with the First Lord."

Immediately after the outbreak of war, and whilst Prince Louis of Battenberg was still First Sea Lord, a War Staff Group was formed at the Admiralty. At Lord Fisher's instance this Staff Group was "greatly strengthened" in November, 1914, and "became still more the supreme and isolated centre of Naval war direction." From that time onwards it consisted of the First Lord, the First Sea Lord, the Chief of the Staff (Vice-Admiral Sir Henry Oliver), Admiral of the Fleet Sir Arthur Wilson, the Secretary to the Board (Sir Graham Greene) and the Naval Secretary (Commodore de Bartolomé). The Second Sea Lord (Admiral Sir Frederick Hamilton), who was previously included in the War Staff Group, ceased to be a member of that body.

The creation of a War Staff Group inevitably tended to diminish the authority and to minimise the collective activity of the Board of Admiralty. The meetings of the Board were less frequent than before the war. In 1913, Mr. Churchill being then First Lord, twenty-four meetings were held. From August 4th, 1914, to May 17th, 1915, when a change in the constitution of the Board took place, only twelve meetings were held. The frequency or infrequency of the official meetings of the Board afford, however, little or no real indication of the influence and authority exercised by its members, either collectively or individually. The functions of the Board, in its collective capacity, have never formed the subject of any very precise definition. The Second Sea Lord (Sir Frederick Hamilton) said: "There was considerable misapprehension always as to what the precise powers of the Board were. The popular notion, I fancy, is that the Board are severally and collectively responsible for anything that takes place, or any measures that are decided upon. In theory that may be very well, but in practice I doubt if it has ever been the case. Although undoubtedly the Board is collectively responsible for any large questions of policy ... it is very difficult to say where a thing ceases to be a matter of detail and becomes a large question of policy."

In point of fact, the position occupied by the Junior Lords of the Admiralty depends almost wholly on the attitude assumed towards them by the First Lord, and, in a minor degree, by the First Sea Lord. The former especially can, at his will, utilise their services in matters lying outside their purely departmental duties, or he can decline to do so. Mr. McKenna informed us that, during the time he was First Lord of the Admiralty, the Board was habitually consulted on all important matters. He stated that in practice he never found any difficulty in harmonising the sole responsibility of the First Lord with the collective responsibility of the Board. "If," he added, "I were First Lord of the Admiralty and I did not consult my Board but consulted expert advisers, I should suggest to the Prime Minister that the Board ought to be changed. The expert advisers to whom the First Lord would naturally look would be his Board."

Sir Graham Greene informed us that from time to time a good deal of discontent had existed at the Admiralty owing to the dubious positions occupied by the Junior Sea Lords. On being asked whether this discontent was especially acute at the period with which we are dealing, he replied: "It may have been felt rather more keenly at that time, because there were two very active and strong personalities in the position of First Lord and First Sea Lord."

There can, indeed, be no doubt that, at the commencement of the war, the Junior Sea Lords resented the position in which they were placed. None of them were consulted about the Dardanelles Expedition.

The Second Sea Lord, Sir Frederick Hamilton, though generally of opinion that the Board of Admiralty had "a right to give their views on large matters of policy," did not complain of the treatment the Board received in the special case of the Dardanelles. He considered that that was "a matter for the Cabinet to decide." The Third Sea Lord (Rear-Admiral Tudor) said that the only opportunity he had of expressing an opinion on the subject was in the course of an informal conversation with Mr. Churchill. He added that his action "was not welcomed and it had no effect."

The Fourth Sea Lord (Commodore Lambert) testified to the fact that the Board had not been consulted about the Dardanelles Expedition, and expressed an opinion that "it would have been a wise and proper subject for the Board's discussion."

On November 22nd, 1915, the Junior Sea Lords addressed collectively a Minute to the present First Lord (Mr. Arthur Balfour), in which they said:

"The principle on which the Order in Council is based that the supremacy of the First Lord is complete and unassailable has been pushed too far, and has tended to imperil and at some future time may again tend to imperil national safety ... The present time may not be the proper one for effecting drastic changes, but of this we are certain, it is the proper and opportune moment to again call the attention of the First Lord to these matters and to express our conviction that had the naval members of the Board been regularly and collectively consulted on large questions of war policy during the progress of the present naval campaign, some at least of the events which the Empire does at this moment deplore so bitterly would not have happened, and that until the authority and responsibility of the Sea Lords is enlarged and defined, there will be no adequate assurance that similar disasters will not recur in the future."

It should be added that in answer to a Minute addressed to him by the Junior Lords on May 18th Mr. Churchill wrote:—

"I agree that the four Sea Lords should be more fully consulted on large questions of War policy as apart from the day to day conduct of the War, where action must proceed easily and rapidly. But neither Prince Louis of Battenberg nor Lord Fisher were in favour of this practice, considering that War plans and War policy lay wholly in the domain of the First Sea Lord, with the First Lord directly over him exercising supreme executive power. It would appear desirable in future that the War situation should be reviewed each week by the naval members of the Board under the Presidency of the First Lord."

Lord Fisher does not, however, appear to have concurred in this view. In the course of the evidence which he gave before us, he said: "With regard to the other Sea Lords, they were tremendously occupied with their business in providing the personnel and stores and other things for the Fleet. I think it would have been a very great pity to have taken them away from their proper duties to have sat round that table."

It is thus abundantly clear that, although no formal and official change was made, the spirit in which the business of the Admiralty was conducted underwent a great transformation immediately after the outbreak of the war. The Board of Admiralty sank into insignificance, its place being taken by the War Staff Group. The Board was, even to a less extent than previously, able to assume any "collective responsibility" for the general conduct of affairs. The individual members of the Board were not kept well-informed of passing events. They were not consulted before the naval attack on the Dardanelles was made.

It is clear that Mr. Asquith was ill-informed as regards the methods under which Admiralty business was conducted when he stated to the Commission that the Members of the War Council "were entitled to assume" that any view laid before them by the First Lord of the Admiralty "was the considered opinion of the Board of Admiralty as a whole."

∘∞⊗∞∘

The War Office

The superior administration of the War Office is regulated by Letters Patent, dated February 6th, 1904, and by various Orders in Council issued in 1904, 1909 and 1910. Of these, the most important is the Order dated August 10th, 1904.

As in the case of the Admiralty, the Secretary of State is solely responsible to the Crown and to Parliament for "all the business of the Army Council."

The Council consists of:—

A first Military Member, the Chief of the
General Staff.

A second Military Member, the Adjutant-
General.

A third Military Member, the Quartermaster-
General.

A fourth Military Member, the Master-General
of the Ordnance.

A Finance Member.

A Civil Member.

The Secretary of the War Office is also Secretary
to the Army Council.

All the members of the Council are responsible
to the Secretary of State for the performance of such
duties as he may from time to time assign to them, the
duties assigned to each member being specified in
King's Regulations, 1914, Appendix IV.

In consequence of the illness and subsequent
death, in October, 1914, of Sir Charles Douglas, Sir
James Wolfe Murray became Chief of the Imperial
General Staff almost immediately after the war commenced. Otherwise, no changes took place in so far
as the Military members of the Army Council were
concerned. Sir Henry Sclater remained Adjutant-
General, Sir John Cowans Quartermaster-General,
and Sir Stanley Von Donop Master-General of the
Ordnance.

Neither did any formal change take place in the
duties and responsibilities of the Council. Viscount
Haldane has informed us that, during the time he was

Secretary of State for War, formal meetings of the Council were not of frequent occurrence, that they were usually held merely to register decisions which had already been taken, and that the informal were of far greater importance than the formal meetings. So far as outward form was concerned, the practice adopted by Lord Kitchener constituted no innovation on the practice which prevailed under his predecessors.

On the other hand, on Lord Kitchener's becoming Secretary of State for War considerable changes had taken place in the military personnel at the War Office, and more important changes were introduced by him in the methods of administration. As regards personnel, according to an arrangement which Sir Reginald Brade informed us had been made previous to the outbreak of war, several of the most important members of the General Staff left the War Office and assumed commands or Staff appointments in the field. Numerous changes were also made amongst the junior members of the Staff.

Mr. Winston Churchill, in speaking of the relations between the War Office and the Admiralty, said: "All the principal officers we were accustomed to work with went off to the war, and a new staff came in."

As regards administrative methods, we think it is much to be regretted that the principles of the devolution of authority and responsibility upon which the War Office system was based were ignored by Lord Kitchener. All the evidence laid before us points to the conclusion that Lord Kitchener was not in the habit of consulting his subordinates, that he frequently gave orders over the heads of the Chiefs of Departments and sometimes without the knowledge of the Chief of the General Staff, and, in fact, that he centralised the whole administration of the War Office in his own hands.

Sir James Murray stated that that portion of the Field Service Regulations which deals with the duties of the Chief of the General Staff were "practically non-existent." On being asked whether he considered that Lord Kitchener centralised too much authority in his own person, he replied, "Yes, I do undoubtedly," and he added that the excessive centralisation of which he complained "was due not to the system, but to the personality of the individual who was Secretary of State."

General Callwell, the Director of Military Operations, stated that "the real reason why the General Staff practically ceased to exist was because it was not consulted." He added that, so far as he was aware, Lord Kitchener never "conferred with anyone very much." General Callwell considered that the extreme centralisation practised "did not tend to the smooth working of the machine."

At a later period of the war, an Order in Council was issued restoring the power of the Chief of the Imperial General Staff which had been allowed to lapse. Sir Reginald Brade, on being asked why this Order was issued, replied, "I think the idea was that Lord Kitchener was in the habit of sending on his own orders in regard to operations, and that he did not ask, or disregarded, the advice of the officers of the General Staff. I think that was the object of it. I do not say that was the fact, but that was understood to be what happened—why that Order in Council was passed."

There can, in fact, be no doubt that the principle of centralisation was pushed to an extreme point by Lord Kitchener. It proved eminently successful during the minor operations in the Soudan, which he conducted with conspicuous skill. But it was unsuitable to a stronger force than that which Lord Kitchener commanded in the Soudan or to operations on so large a scale as those in which this country has recently been engaged. Its result was to throw on the hands of one man an amount of work with which no individual, however capable, could hope to cope successfully.

It will thus be seen that, almost immediately after the outbreak of war, the following important changes took place:—

1. The ordinary functions of the Cabinet practically lapsed in so far as the conduct of the war was concerned.
2. A War Council, with supreme powers, was instituted to take the place of the Committee of Imperial Defence.
3. The consultative functions which would ordinarily have been performed by the Board of Admiralty were transferred to a new body termed the "War Staff Group."
4. Some important changes were made in the

personnel of the War Office. The staff and administrative functions of the office were practically centralised in the hands of one man.

Narrative of events from August 1914 until January 1st, 1915

It had for long been recognised by the naval and military authorities of this country that any attack on the Dardanelles would be an operation which presented very great difficulties. In 1878, Admiral Hornby, on the occasion of a naval demonstration made, with the consent of the Ottoman Government, before Constantinople, wrote a report on the subject.

In 1906–07, at a time when the relations between

the British Government and the Porte, the Turkish Parliament, were somewhat strained, the matter came under consideration. Both the General Staff of the War Office and the Director of Naval Intelligence at the Admiralty were alive to the great risks which would be involved even in a joint naval and military enterprise against the Gallipoli Peninsula. In a Memorandum, dated December 19th, 1906, prepared by the General Staff, the following passage occurs: "Military opinion, looking at the question from the point of view of coast defence, will be in entire agreement with the naval view that unaided action by the Fleet, bearing in mind the risks involved, is much to be deprecated."

Further, the works of Mr. Julian Corbett and other authorities had familiarised the general public with the view that it had become almost a fundamental principle of naval strategy that the attack of ships on forts, without military aid, was rarely productive of satisfactory results. The experience gained at Port Arthur, Santiago, Wei-Hai-Wei and elsewhere was held to confirm this view.

It was contended that the improvements made in modern artillery, the experience recently gained in Belgium, in connection especially with the bombardment of Liège, Namur and Antwerp, and the use of aircraft, had rendered any analogy between the present and the past of little value. *A fortiori*, the experience gained by Admiral Duckworth in 1807 was valueless. We shall revert presently to this subject, with a view to discussing how far these precedents were applicable to the case of the recent attack on the Dardanelles.

Towards the end of August 1914 Mr. Churchill formed the opinion that Turkey would join Germany and the other Central Powers. On the 1st September he wrote privately to General Douglas, who was then Chief of the Imperial General Staff, in the following terms:—

"I arranged with Lord Kitchener yesterday that two officers from the Admiralty should meet two officers from the D.M.O's. Department of the War Office to-day to examine and work out a plan for the seizure, by means of a Greek Army of adequate strength, of the Gallipoli Peninsula, with a view to admitting a British Fleet to the Sea of Marmora.

In his absence I would ask you to give the necessary directions, as the matter is urgent, and Turkey may make war on us at any moment.

The meeting can take place either here or at the War Office as soon as you can arrange with our Chief of the Staff. I will myself explain verbally to the Committee the points on which His Majesty's Government desire information."

On September 3rd General Callwell, the Director of Military Operations, wrote a Memorandum on the subject, in which he said that—

"it ought to be clearly understood that an attack upon the Gallipoli Peninsula from the sea side

(outside the Straits) is likely to prove an
extremely difficult operation of war."

He referred to the discussions which had taken place
in 1906–07, and expressed the opinion that it would
not be justifiable to undertake the operation with an
army of less than 60,000 men.

On October 31st, Turkey declared war. On
November 3rd, the outer forts of the Dardanelles
were bombarded for about ten minutes. The object of
this bombardment was merely to find out, by a practical test, the effective range of the guns of the Turkish
forts.

Sir Henry Jackson has expressed the opinion, in
which we concur, that this bombardment was a mis-
take, as it was calculated to place the Turks on the
alert. Commodore de Bartolomé characterised this
demonstration as "unfortunate." The orders to bombard emanated solely from the Admiralty and the War
Council was not consulted.

On November 25th, the idea of making a serious
attack on the Dardanelles was discussed at a meeting
of the War Council. Mr. Churchill said that the best
way to defend Egypt was to make an attack on some
part of the coast of Asiatic Turkey, and, as an extension
of this idea, he suggested an attack on the Gallipoli
Peninsula, which, if successful, would give us the control of the Dardanelles and enable us to dictate terms
at Constantinople. He added that this would be a very
difficult operation and would require a large force.
Lord Kitchener agreed that it might become neces-

sary to make a diversion by an attack on the Turkish communications, but considered that the moment had not yet arrived for doing so.

A proposal to collect transport, horse-boats, etc., at some British port in the Mediterranean was also discussed. The idea at the time was that a feint attack might be made on the Gallipoli Peninsula, in order to convey the impression that a landing was intended there, whereas the real point of attack would be made at some other point on the Turkish coast. This proposal was rejected owing to the shortage of tonnage for mercantile purposes, due partly to military demands. It was thought undesirable to aggravate this evil.

Nevertheless, on November 30th, Vice-Admiral Sir Henry Oliver, the Chief of the Staff at the Admiralty, again proposed that transport should be collected in Egypt sufficient to convey one division. Mr. Churchill passed this suggestion on to the War Office, adding that he thought transport should be collected, or kept in readiness at short notice sufficient to convey 40,000 men. Lord Kitchener at once replied: "I will give the Admiralty full notice. I do not think transports need be detained in Egypt yet."

On receipt of this reply, Mr. Churchill "put the project on one side and thought no more of it for the time." Nevertheless, horse-boats continued to be despatched to Alexandria whenever the occasion was offered, "in case the War Office should, at a future stage wish to undertake joint naval and military operation in the Eastern Mediterranean."

January 2nd–January 13th 1915

Thus matters stood until January 2nd, 1915, when a very important telegram, which materially affected the situation, was received from His Majesty's Ambassador at Petrograd. In this telegram it was represented that the Russians were being somewhat hardly pressed in the Caucasus, and a hope was expressed, on behalf of the Russian Government, that, in order to relieve this pressure, a demonstration against the Turks would be made in some other quarter.

On the following day (January 3rd) a reply was sent to the Ambassador, authorising him to assure the Russian Government that a demonstration would be made against the Turks, but stating it was feared that any such action would be unlikely seriously to affect the withdrawal of enemy troops in the Caucasus. This telegram was sent from the Foreign Office, but it was drafted at the War Office. Lord Grey explained to us that the Foreign Office merely acted as a medium of communication. But it is not on this account to be inferred that Lord Grey in any way disapproved of the telegram. On the contrary, he held that "When an Ally appealed for assistance we were bound to do what we could," and that it would have had a bad effect if that assistance had been refused.

Mr. Asquith thinks that he did not see this telegram before it was sent, but it must not be by any means inferred on that account that he would not have approved of its despatch if he had seen it.

Mr. Churchill did not see the telegram before it was sent, but he had a long conversation with Lord Kitchener on January 2nd, after the receipt of the Petrograd message, and he thinks that Lord Kitchener's reply was the outcome of that conversation.

This, therefore, was the first phase in the whole transaction. By January 3rd His Majesty's Government was pledged to make a demonstration against the Turks. The time and method of making that demonstration were, as yet, wholly undecided.

On January 2nd, Mr. Churchill received the following private letter from Lord Kitchener:

"I do not see that we can do anything that will seriously help the Russians in the Caucasus. The Turks are evidently withdrawing most of their troops from Adrianople and using them to reinforce their army against Russia, probably sending them by the Black Sea .... We have no troops to land anywhere .... The only place that a demonstration might have some effect in stopping reinforcements going East would be the Dardanelles .... We shall not be ready for anything big for some months."

It will be convenient to interrupt the thread of the narrative at this point in order to deal briefly with the question, which has formed the subject of much discussion, of who was primarily responsible for originating the proposal to make a purely naval attack on the Dardanelles.

In considering this question, it has to be remembered that Mr. Churchill himself, in common with all the experts who were consulted at the time, as well as those who gave their opinions subsequently, was greatly in favour of a joint naval and military attack rather than one conducted by ships alone.

Lord Fisher, in giving his evidence, spoke of the "purely naval operation at the Dardanelles" as "Lord Kitchener's proposal," and condemned it in strong terms. He based this opinion on Lord Kitchener's letter to Mr. Churchill of January 2nd, quoted in the preceding paragraph. We are unable to concur in Lord Fisher's view. Lord Kitchener suggested and pressed for a demonstration, but that did not necessarily involve a deliberate attempt to force a passage. The proper conclusion seems to be that when a demonstration appeared to be necessary the First Lord thought it was possible to convert and extend that demonstration into an attempt to force a passage, and took the steps which are detailed in the immediately succeeding paragraph.

On a review of the whole of the evidence on this point, a fairly safe conjecture may be made of what was passing through Lord Kitchener's mind early in January. It has to be borne in mind that the question which both Lord Kitchener and the Government generally had to decide was not whether the attack on the Dardanelles should be amphibious or purely naval, but whether, owing to the impossibility of supplying an adequate military force, any attack at all should be undertaken, or whether, on the other hand, the operation should be limited to a mere demonstration. Lord Kitchener was, without doubt, strongly impressed with both the military and political necessity of acting on the appeal made by the Russian Government. The new army he was creating was not yet ready. He had to provide for home defence, to which he attached the utmost importance. He was most unwilling to withdraw a single man from France. The views entertained by Mr. Churchill at the time as to the prospects of success of a purely naval operation, were, as we shall presently show, somewhat more optimistic than was warranted by the opinions of the experts.

Under these circumstances, Lord Kitchener grasped, perhaps rather too eagerly, at the proposal to act through the agency of the Fleet alone, though he recognised the objections to any such undertaking, but it cannot with justice or accuracy be said that the responsibility for proposing the adoption of this course rested with him. It rested rather on the First Lord.

We should here mention that at a somewhat late stage of our Inquiry, Sir George Arthur intimated to us that he was in a position to give evidence bearing upon the question of the extent to which Lord Kitchener was primarily responsible for the initiation of the Dardanelles expedition. He subsequently handed in a statement descriptive of a conversation which he had held with Lord Kitchener, and which was to the following effect:—

Lord Kitchener stated that "at a conference to which he was invited by the First Lord of the Admiralty, when the passage of the Dardanelles was the subject of discussion, he protested vigorously against any such an undertaking by the Navy without very strong and very carefully prepared support from and co-operation with the Army"; that the First Lord had stated that the experience of the past was no longer admissible by reason of the "marvellous potentialities of the 'Queen Elizabeth,'" which ship was about to be sent to the Dardanelles; that Lord Kitchener admitted that "he had no expert knowledge of the 'Queen Elizabeth,' and was therefore not in a position to contradict or depreciate the opinion as to her astounding effectiveness, which the First Lord had alleged would revolutionise all previous estimates of naval warfare"; and that he "contented himself with renewing his protest in which he was sure that he voiced all military opinion; but he said also that his inevitable uneasiness would have been considerably diminished had he been able to satisfy himself that the First Lord's confidence both in the 'Queen Elizabeth' and in the success of his plan was wholly and whole-heartedly shared by his chief naval advisers."

Much depends upon the date upon which this conversation occurred. Sir George Arthur was unable to give a precise date, but it resulted from his examination that without any doubt it was held about the same time as the War Council which took place on May 14th. At that Council, indeed, Lord Kitchener expressed himself in terms somewhat similar to those used by Sir George Arthur. He read the following statement:—

"When the Admiralty proposed to force the passage of the Dardanelles by means of the Fleet alone, I doubted whether the attempt would succeed, but was led to believe it possible by the First Lord's statements of the power of the 'Queen Elizabeth' and the Admiralty Staff paper showing how the operation was to be conducted ... I regret that I was led to agree in the enterprise by the statements made, particularly as to the power of the 'Queen Elizabeth,' of which I had no means of judging." It will be seen, therefore, that Sir George Arthur's evidence has no direct bearing upon the immediate subject of our Inquiry, namely, the opinions Lord Kitchener expressed during the period of origin and inception, which we consider to have closed on March 23rd, 1915.

We also called Major-General Sir Stanley Von Donop and Mr. H. J. Creedy, one of Lord Kitchener's private secretaries, to give evidence on the same point, but neither added any material information to the facts which were already in our possession.

To resume the narrative of events. On January 3rd, 1915, the following telegram was despatched from the Admiralty to Vice-Admiral Carden:—

"Do you think that it is a practicable operation to force the Dardanelles by the use of ships alone?

It is assumed that older battleships would be employed, that they would be furnished with mine sweepers and that they would be preceded by colliers or other merchant vessels as sweepers and bumpers.

The importance of the results would justify severe loss. Let me know what your views are."

On January 5th, Vice-Admiral Carden replied to the Admiralty telegram of the 3rd, in the following terms:—

"I do not think that the Dardanelles can be rushed, but they might be forced by extended operations with a large number of ships."

In the course of the evidence given before us, Vice-Admiral Carden was asked to explain more fully what he meant by saying that the Dardanelles "might be forced." In reply, he stated: "I did not mean distinctly that they could be forced. I had it in my mind that it was impossible to form a real opinion on the subject until one had destroyed the outer forts at the entrance, and was able to get inside and actually find out the extent of the gun defences, of the mine field and the extent of the movable armament on both sides of the Straits." It is to be observed, however, that no reservation of this sort was made in the telegram sent to the Admiralty on January 5th.

On January 6th, the following telegram was sent from the First Lord to Vice-Admiral Carden:—

"High authorities here concur in your opinion. Forward detailed particulars showing what force would be required for extended operations. How do you think it should be employed, and what results could be gained?"

The wording of this telegram is certainly open to criticism. We shall deal presently with the views entertained by the various authorities at the Admiralty. Here we need only remark that at the time Lord Fisher was by far the highest naval authority at the Admiralty, and that, in the absence of any explicit statement to the contrary, Vice-Admiral Carden would naturally suppose that he was included amongst those who concurred in the view set forth in his telegram of January 5th.

This, in fact, is what actually happened. Vice-Admiral Carden, on being asked "What high authorities did you think were meant?" replied: "Well, I knew that Lord Fisher was there and Sir Henry Jackson. I thought it was either or both of them." Now, Lord Fisher agreed with the telegram to Vice-Admiral Carden of January 3rd, but he does not think he was shown the telegram of the 6th before it was sent. "I think," he said in his evidence, "that I should have objected to that, and asked him (Mr. Churchill) to word it in some other way. Naturally, Carden would think I was in it, would he not?" Mr. Churchill, on the other hand, did not wish it to be inferred that Lord Fisher was included amongst the "high authorities." "I do not," he said, "think it would have been fair to include Lord Fisher then." As regards Sir Henry Jackson, to whose supposed concurrence Vice-Admiral Carden alluded in his evidence, he stated to the Commission that he could not remember whether he was or was not consulted before the telegram of January 6th was despatched. But Mr. Churchill, in reply to a question put to him by Mr. Clyde, stated that when he spoke of "high authorities" he meant only Sir Henry Jackson and Admiral Oliver, both of whom had expressed their opinions to him verbally.

On January 3rd, simultaneously with the despatch of the telegram to Vice-Admiral Carden, Mr. Churchill requested Sir Henry Jackson to prepare a memorandum on the project, which Sir Henry Jackson described as a "note on forcing the Passages of the Dardanelles and Bosphorus by the Allied Fleets in order to destroy the Turko-German squadron and threaten Constantinople without military co-operation." On January 5th, Sir Henry Jackson wrote a memorandum, which was not, however, received by Mr. Churchill till some time after the despatch of the telegram of the 6th to Vice-Admiral Carden. In this memorandum, Sir Henry Jackson did not pronounce any definite opinion either for or against the attack on the Dardanelles. He only dwelt on the minimum force required to undertake the operation, on the losses which would probably be involved in any attempt to "reach the Straits," to which he was strongly opposed, and on the necessity of providing a large supply of ammunition.

He added: "Assuming the enemy squadron destroyed and the batteries rushed, they would be open to the fire of field artillery and infantry, and to torpedo attack at night, with no store ships with ammunition, and no retreat without re-engaging the shore batteries, unless these had been destroyed when forcing the passage. Though they might dominate the city and inflict enormous damage, their position would not be an enviable one, unless there were a large military force to occupy the town. Strategically, such a diversion would only be carried out when the object to be gained was commensurate with the loss the Fleet would sustain in forcing the passage. The actual capture of Constantinople would be worth a considerable loss; but its bombardment alone would not greatly affect the distant military operations; and even if it surrendered, it could not be occupied and held without troops, and would probably result in indiscriminate massacres."

On January 11th, Vice-Admiral Carden replied to the telegram sent to him from the Admiralty on the 6th. Four operations, he said, were possible. These were:

(*a*) The destruction of defences at the entrance to the Dardanelles.

(*b*) Action inside the Straits, so as to clear the defences up to and including Cephez Point battery N.8.

(*c*) Destruction of defences of the Narrows.

(*d*) Sweeping of a clear channel through the mine field and advance through the Narrows, followed by a reduction of the forts further up, and advance into the Sea of Marmora.

He estimated that it would take a month to carry out all these operations.

This telegram, Mr. Churchill informed us, "made a great impression on every one who saw it. It was in its details an entirely novel proposition." We understand that the novelty of the proposition consisted in the abandonment of any attempt to rush the Dardanelles, and in the substitution in its place of a scheme by which the forts would be methodically attacked and destroyed one by one. "That, of course," Mr. Churchill said, "squared with the impression produced in many people's minds by the destruction of the strong forts on land by the German heavy artillery."

On January 15th, Sir Henry Jackson recorded his opinion on Admiral Carden's proposal. His memorandum began with the following remark: "Concur generally in his plans." After dealing at some length with the detailed proposals, Sir Henry Jackson concluded by saying: "I would suggest (*a*) might be approved at once, as the experience gained would be useful." He did not recommend the undertaking of (*c*) and (*d*) unless the experience gained from (*a*) and (*b*) justified it. It will be observed that this Memorandum is dated January 15th, that is to say, two days after the meeting of the War Council on January 13th, to which we shall presently allude.

Sir Henry Jackson insisted strongly in the evidence which he gave before us that, in writing his Memorandum of January 15th, he agreed to an attack on the outer forts and nothing more. He did not consider that an attempt made by the Fleet alone to get through the Dardanelles was "a feasible operation." He thought that "it would be a mad thing to do." He denied the accuracy of the statement made by Mr. Churchill that he, Sir Henry Oliver, and Vice-Admiral Carden "were all agreed." He thought that Mr. Churchill was "very much more sanguine" than they were. But nothing of this sort was put on record at the time.

The concurrence expressed by Sir Henry Jackson in his Memorandum of January 15th with the whole of Vice-Admiral Carden's plans is unqualified save by the expression of an opinion that only the first item of the programme, viz., that which involved the destruction of the outer forts, should be approved at once, with a view to gaining experience. The explanation of Sir Henry Jackson's reticent attitude is probably to be found in the answer which he gave to a question addressed to him by Mr. Fisher to the effect that it was not part of his duty to "unduly interfere with the naval policy except if he were invited to do so by some superior." He also said in the course of his evidence: "It was not for me to decide. I had no responsibilities whatever as to the decision. I had no responsibilities except just for the staff work which I did." He was consulted before the initial telegram of January 3rd was sent to Vice-Admiral Carden and expressed his concurrence with its contents.

Sir Henry Oliver would greatly have preferred to wait until the army was ready, when a joint naval and military attack might have been made. But he, nevertheless, acquiesced in the naval attack. He thought "we should push on slowly till either we overcame the enemy's defence, or till the enemy's defence brought us to a standstill." Further, he stated, "I think the view was that we would go on, and by the time that we had got over the initial difficulties the military force would have been provided."

Commodore de Bartolomé's opinion was expressed before the Commission in the following terms: "My impression was always that the naval members would much sooner have had a combined operation, and that they only agreed to a purely naval operation on the understanding that we could always draw back—that there should be no question of what is known as forcing the Dardanelles."

We shall refer presently more particularly to the views entertained by Lord Fisher and Sir Arthur Wilson. Here it will be sufficient to state that as regards the other members of the Admiralty staff who were consulted, all would have preferred a joint naval and military attack, but none dissented from the bombardment of the outer forts. Their concurrence was not apparently very cordial; at the same time there can be no doubt that it was given. They were apparently much influenced by the consideration that the matter could be reconsidered after the results of bombarding the outer forts had been ascertained.

The meeting of the War Council on January 13th

Before proceeding any further, it may be desirable to describe briefly the military and political situation which existed at the moment when the very important meeting of the War Council took place on January 13th.

At that time the rival armies in the Western theatre of war had reached a state of deadlock. The desperate attacks made by the Germans on the British position at Ypres had been repulsed with great losses to the enemy. It seemed tolerably clear that no attempts to break through the French and British lines could prove successful. On the other hand, the Allies were not in sufficiently superior strength to justify any hope that they would speedily break through the German lines.

In the Eastern theatre of war, the Austrians had sustained some serious defeats. But the Russian position, though for the moment satisfactory, was in reality somewhat precarious, owing to a lack of munitions and inadequate railway communications, both being defects which could not be speedily corrected.

In Serbia the position was very menacing. The attitude likely to be assumed by Bulgaria was the dominating factor in the Balkan Peninsula. All attempts to secure the military co-operation of the Balkan States had failed. "Diplomacy," as Lord Grey explained to us, "was perfectly useless without military success." Bulgaria was still neutral, but the proclivities of its ruler were well known. It was thought that a decisive military success on the part of the Allies would prove the most effective method for securing the continued maintenance of his neutrality. Italy was still neutral.

It was under such circumstances that the British Government had to consider in what direction a blow could most effectively be delivered, in order at one and the same time to relieve the pressure on Russia and to deter Bulgaria from active adherence to the cause of the Central Powers.

We do not think it necessary, neither, so long as

the war lasts, would it be at all advisable, to deal in a report intended for publication with the alternative projects which at the time came under the consideration of the Government. It will suffice to say that for various reasons, some political and others either naval or military, all, save the proposal to make an attempt on the Dardanelles, were rejected. The entrance of the Allied Fleets into the Sea of Marmora, followed, as would probably have been the case, by the occupation of Constantinople, would, it cannot be doubted, have exercised a profound effect on the future course of the war. The advantages capable of being secured by success in this enterprise were, indeed, so obvious that it is unnecessary to dwell on them at any length. But they may be briefly mentioned.

It would, without doubt, have finally deterred Bulgaria from joining the cause of the Central Powers. It would have enabled the Russian Government to import the war material of which they stood greatly in need. It would, to the great advantage of Russia herself and of the rest of the world, have enabled Russian agricultural products to be exported. Finally, it would have gone far to settle a question which has been a constant source of trouble to Europe for centuries past. These advantages were so great that they may possibly have produced a tendency on the part of the members of the War Council to be governed by them to an excessive degree, and to neglect unduly the sole question which was really open to discussion, namely, the advisability of undertaking at that time a purely naval enterprise. That question was obviously one on which only the opinions expressed by naval and military experts would be of any value. It becomes, therefore, essential to consider what were the views entertained and expressed on January 13th by the naval and military advisers of the Government.

The principal and, indeed, the sole adviser of the Government on military questions was Lord Kitchener. The actual proposal on which Lord Kitchener had to give an opinion at the meeting held on January 13th was thus summarised in Sir Maurice Hankey's notes of the proceedings of the Council: "Mr. Churchill said he had interchanged telegrams with Vice-Admiral Carden, the Commander-in-Chief in the Mediterranean, in regard to the possibilities of a naval attack on the Dardanelles. The sense of Admiral Carden's reply was that it was impossible to rush the Dardanelles, but that, in his opinion, it might be possible to demolish the forts one by one. To this end Admiral Carden had submitted a plan.

"His proposal was first to concentrate his fire on the entrance forts. When they were demolished he would proceed to deal with the inner forts, attacking them from the Straits and from the seaward side of the Gallipoli Peninsula. This plan was based on the fact that the Dardanelles forts are armed mainly with old guns of only thirty-five calibre. These would be outranged by the guns of the ships, which would effect their object without coming into range. Three modern ships, carrying the heaviest guns, would be required for reducing some of the more modern works, and about twelve old battleships would deal with the remainder. These could now be spared for the task without reducing our strength in the main theatre of war. Among others, he mentioned the 'Triumph', 'Swiftsure', 'Goliath', 'Glory', and 'Canopus', all of which had been employed hitherto for trade protection. Four of the Majestic class, which were to have been 'scrapped', their 12-inch guns being utilised for monitors, could also be made available, though this would entail a delay in the completion of the monitors. Two battle-cruisers were, he said, already in the Mediterranean. The new battle-cruiser 'Queen Elizabeth' was already to be sent to Gibraltar for gun trials, and it would be feasible to allow her to conduct her trials against the Dardanelles forts, instead of against a target.

"The Admiralty were studying the question, and believed that a plan could be made for systematically reducing all the forts within a few weeks. Once the forts were reduced the minefields would be cleared, and the Fleet would proceed up to Constantinople and destroy the 'Goeben' [*Turkish battleship*]. They would have nothing to fear from field guns or rifles, which would be merely an inconvenience."

Sir Maurice Hankey then records:—

"Lord Kitchener thought the plan was worth trying. We could leave off the bombardment if it did not prove effective."

Lord Fisher said nothing, but it is essential to inquire fully as to what views he really entertained at this moment. He occupied a position of great responsibility. It is highly probable that if either Lord Kitchener or Lord Fisher had, from the first, expressed, on technical grounds, strong objections to the attack on the Dardanelles, the project would have been abandoned, and it may be regarded as quite certain that, under this hypothesis, the plan would have been much more carefully examined than appears to have been the case.

Lord Crewe, in the course of his evidence, stated: "I should be very sorry indeed to state what the effect would have been on our minds if Lord Fisher had made a full statement of his actual objections from the naval point of view, speaking as First Sea Lord. Of course then the Government would have had to consider whether the political advantages were worth the risk. I cannot say what the ultimate decision would have been, but I have not the least doubt that it would have altered the form and manner of our consideration of the whole subject to a great extent."

Lord Grey also said: "Of course if we had thought that we were forcing upon naval officers an operation which they were reluctant to undertake, I think we should not have contemplated it for a moment; but we understood that the naval officers who were on the spot who were to carry it out, and who had advised about it, were in favour of it, and we were attracted by what we were told about big guns and forts, and so forth, and we were prepared to authorise the operation being proceeded with."

Lord Fisher made a very full statement to us of

the views which he entertained. Mr. Churchill also
dwelt at length on this subject, and allusion has been
made to it by many other witnesses. We think that we
can now confidently describe the attitude he assumed
both on January 13th and at later periods. It is certain
that Lord Fisher did not underrate the importance of
the Dardanelles enterprise. On January 3rd, in a "private and personal" letter to Mr. Churchill, Lord Fisher
said: "I consider the attack on Turkey holds the field."
He then sketched out the broad out-lines of a general
plan of operations in the Eastern theatre of war. This
plan involved, *inter alia*, the withdrawal of a considerable force from France, and was, therefore, at all events
for the time being, incapable of execution. Lord
Fisher, in fact, like all other experts, both naval and
military, was in favour of a combined attack, but not
of action by the Fleet alone. It is certain that, from the
very first, he disliked the purely naval operation, but
it is especially to be observed that his main objection
was not based upon the impracticability of the
scheme, considered on its own merits, but on the
strong opinion which he entertained that the British
Fleet could be better employed elsewhere. All the evidence we have received, including that of Lord Fisher
himself, tends to confirm the perfect accuracy of the
following statement made to us by Mr. Asquith:—

"As I understand, because I had frequent conversations with him, Lord Fisher's objection to the
Dardanelles operations was not so much a technical
objection upon naval grounds. It is quite true that, I
think throughout, he thought the best chance of suc-

cess for such an operation would have been a combined operation in which both the land and sea forces were engaged; but Lord Fisher's main objection, at least the one he always impressed on me, was not based in any degree upon the technical or naval merits or demerits of the Dardanelles operations, but upon the fact that he preferred another objective ... So far as I understood, from all the conversations I had with him, it was much more upon that ground than upon any specific objection on what you may call technical naval grounds that he was opposed to it."

We have already mentioned that in our present Report we propose only to deal with events which occurred up to March 23rd, but it may be advisable so far to forestall the contents of our future Report as to say that throughout the whole of the proceedings Lord Fisher consistently maintained the attitude described in the above extract from Mr. Asquith's evidence. He reluctantly acquiesced in the Dardanelles operations so long as he thought they would not seriously interfere with the plans which he wished to carry into execution elsewhere. But when in the month of May he became convinced that the demands made on the Fleet for action in the Dardanelles would prejudice his alternative schemes, he resigned his post at the Admiralty. It should be clearly understood that his resignation was due solely to this cause and not to objections he entertained to the original scheme for attacking the Dardanelles considered exclusively on its own merits. Lord Fisher did, indeed, state in the course of his evidence that he "was dead against the naval operation alone because he knew it must be a failure." He also said, "I must reiterate that as a purely naval operation I think it was doomed to failure." But he did not at the time record any such strongly adverse opinions as these, neither does he appear to have impressed others with the strength of his objections. Lord Grey stated: "We (the Members of the War Council) understood that the naval authorities, who were to be charged with the carrying out of the operation, considered it a practicable operation by naval means alone." Lord Grey "got to know that Lord Fisher did hold views of his own," but he thinks that this fact did not come to his knowledge until after the decision of January 13th had been taken. Mr. Asquith, on being asked in what light he interpreted the views of the experts, replied: "Very favourable. Mr. Churchill told me so, and I thought they were." Further, on being asked whether Lord Fisher had ever given him to understand that from the first he considered that the Dardanelles expedition was "doomed to failure," Mr. Asquith replied: "No, he never said that to me. He would always have preferred a conjoint military and naval operation, but he never said it was doomed to failure; and I do not think he thought it was."

Mr. Churchill said to us: "I think I am entitled to state that it was my impression, and it was the impression of every one present at this meeting of the 13th, that in what I said I carried with me the full agreement of those who were there." It is perhaps somewhat overstating the case to say that Lord Fisher was in "full agreement," but it is undeniable that, by not dissenting, Lord Fisher may reasonably have been held to agree, and that, so far as we have been able to ascertain, he did not, before the meeting, express anything approaching to strong disapproval save on the ground to which we have already alluded, namely, that he feared that the Dardanelles operations would interfere with the execution of other schemes which he favoured. Indeed, on January 12th, Lord Fisher initialled and passed on to the Chief of the Staff the following Minute, which had been written by the First Lord:

> "Secret. Minute by the First Lord to Secretary, First Sea Lord, Chief of Staff. The forcing of the Dardanelles as proposed and the arrival of a squadron strong enough to defeat the Turkish Fleet in the Sea of Marmora would be victory of first importance and change to our advantage the whole situation of the war in the East. It would appear possible to provide the force required by Admiral Carden without weakening the margin necessary in Home waters, as follows."

The details connected with the proposed movements of ships were then given.

Moreover, on January 14th, Lord Fisher concurred with a Memorandum which was sent from the First Lord to the Prime Minister in which the following passage occurs: "The attack on the Dardanelles will require practically our whole available margin. If that attack opens prosperously it will very soon attract to itself the whole attention of the Eastern theatre, and if it succeeds it will produce results which will undoubtedly influence every Mediterranean Power. In these circumstances we strongly advise ... that we should devote ourselves to action in accordance with the third conclusion of the War Council, viz., the methodical forcing of the Dardanelles." We shall have presently to revert to the views entertained both by Lord Fisher and Sir Arthur Wilson when we come to deal with a further meeting of the War Council, which took place on January 28th.

The actual decision arrived at by the War Council on January 13th, after hearing the views expressed by Lord Kitchener and Mr. Churchill—Lord Fisher, Sir Arthur Wilson and Sir James Murray remaining silent—was couched in the following terms:—

"The Admiralty should prepare for a naval expedition in February to bombard and take the Gallipoli Peninsula, with Constantinople as its objective."

It is impossible to read all the evidence, or to study the voluminous papers which have been submitted to us, without being struck with the atmosphere of vagueness and want of precision which seems to have characterised the proceedings of the War Council. We have already mentioned that some of those present at the meetings of the Council left without having any very clear idea of what had or had not been decided. The decision of the Council, taken on January 13th, is another case in point. The Admiralty was to "prepare" for a naval expedition, and nothing more. It would naturally be inferred from the wording of the decision that the matter was to be reconsidered by the Council when the preparations were complete, and after the Admiralty plan was matured. Actual approval of the bombardment was withheld. The following extract from the evidence given by Mr. Asquith will show that this is the way in which he understood the decision:—

"*The Chairman.* Did you understand that it (the decision) was merely provisional, to prepare, but nothing more? It did not pledge you to anything more?

A. No.

Q. You did not think it approved it?

A. No. I think all of us thought this was a very promising operation, and the Admiralty ought to get ready for it.

Q. But nothing more?

A. No, no more than that."

Mr. Churchill apparently considered that the decision of January 13th went further than the approval of mere preparation. Employing Parliamentary metaphor, he likened the meetings of January 13th and 28th respectively to the Second and Third readings of a Bill. "I do not think," he said, "that the meeting of the 13th would be the introduction; it was more than that—it was the approval of a principle, with the general knowledge of how it was to be given effect to."

The statement made by Lord Crewe probably represents with accuracy the manner in which the decision was generally understood by the members of the Council. "I think," he said, in answer to a question which was addressed to him, "I should say that it was approved subject to the occurrence of any unforeseen event which might have made it from one point of view unnecessary."

The following extract from General Callwell's evidence shows how he regarded the decision taken on January 13th. It may, with some confidence, be presumed that General Callwell's views were shared by other officials both at the War Office and the Admiralty.

"*Mr. Clyde.* When the naval operation was undertaken, did you understand it to be an undertaking to force the Dardanelles with ships only?

A. Yes, certainly, to force it gradually.

Q. As undertaken, did you understand it to be anything of the limited character of a demonstration?

A. No, certainly not . . .

Q. In short, you regarded it from the beginning as a definite serious project definitely to force the passage of the Dardanelles?

A. Certainly.

The Chairman. From the early stage in January?

A. Yes, from the very beginning, the 13th January."

The decision taken at this meeting of the Council calls for one further observation. When Mr. Churchill spoke of the "general knowledge" imparted to the Council of how the "principle" which he advocated should be carried into effect, he, without doubt, meant that the force to be employed was to be purely naval. On this point all the witnesses whom we have examined were unanimous.

Thus, Lord Grey said: "My recollection is that it was distinctly said to us that the troops would not be asked for; that if the Navy could not carry out the operation by itself, the operation would not be proceeded with; and that our first consent was given on that understanding; and I gave my consent on that understanding because I was informed—I believed Lord Kitchener's opinion to be—that no troops were available."

The determination to employ ships alone must be considered in connection with the phrase used in the recorded decision taken on January 13th, that the Admiralty, in preparing for the bombardment, was to consider "Constantinople as its objective."

It was from the first recognised by all the naval experts that small bodies of troops would have to be landed on the Gallipoli Peninsula, partly for finally demolishing the forts which had been bombarded by the Fleet, and partly also, in all probability, to attack those batteries which could not effectively be reached by the ships' guns. It is almost inconceivable that any one, whether military, naval or civilian, could have imagined for one moment that Constantinople would be captured without military help on a somewhat large scale. It is clear that by the decision of January 13th, although the War Council only pledged itself for the moment to naval action, they were, in reality, committed to military action on a large scale in the event of the attempt to force the Dardanelles by the Fleet alone proving successful.

We have mentioned that the first phase of these transactions was reached on January 3rd, when the Russian Government was informed that a "demonstration" of some sort would be made against the Turks.

A demonstration may, as Lord Grey pointed out, "of course, not mean active operations at all." The second phase was reached on January 13th. The idea of a mere demonstration, which would not involve active operations, was then definitely abandoned. A decision, which was somewhat variously interpreted, was taken that the Admiralty should "prepare" for an attack on the Gallipoli Peninsula, with the ulterior object of pushing on to Constantinople. The attack was intended to be purely naval, but if successful, in our opinion, necessarily involved, at a somewhat later period, the active co-operation of considerable military forces with the Fleet.

Co-operation with the French; the advantages of a purely naval attack

The first step very wisely taken by the First Lord of the Admiralty after he had received from the War Council a mandate to "prepare" for a bombardment of the Gallipoli Peninsula was to communicate with the French Government with a view to securing the co-operation of the French fleet. M. Augagneur, the French Minister of Marine, visited London. In the course of the discussions which took place with him an arrangement was speedily made as to the sphere of maritime action in the Mediterranean to be assigned respectively to the naval forces of the two countries. The French squadron at the Dardanelles was to be placed under the command of Admiral Carden. The detailed plan of action proposed by the Admiralty was then communicated to the French Government and examined by the Ministry of Marine at Paris [by whom it was accepted.]

The allusion made in M. Augagneur's letter to the possibility of desisting from the naval attack if "insurmountable difficulties" were encountered renders this a convenient opportunity for dwelling at somewhat greater length on this argument, which played an important part in the decision taken at the meeting of the War Council of January 28th, which we are about to describe, and which assumed even greater importance at a later stage of the proceedings.

It may confidently be asserted that anyone conversant with Eastern affairs would have predicted, in January, 1915, that if a serious attack on the Dardanelles was made and if it failed, the result would be to give a shattering blow to British prestige and influence throughout the East. As a matter of fact, the attack failed, but, so far as can at present be judged, the political consequences, although a serious check to British arms was shortly afterwards experienced in Mesopotamia, have been so slight as to be almost inappreciable.

An additional proof is thus furnished of the extreme difficulty experienced by any Western when he endeavours to forecast the ratiocinative processes of the Eastern mind. But this result could not be, and was not, foreseen at the time when the decision had to be taken. Lord Kitchener, as might naturally be expected from his long Eastern experience, was more especially impressed with the harm which would ensue from failure, but although he and others realised the inevitable risk which would have to be run, they thought, in the first instance, that any serious loss of prestige could, in any case, be avoided by desisting from the attack if, after some experience had been gained, the prospect of success was greatly diminished. A great distinction was made between the withdrawal of the fleet and evacuation by a military force when it had once been landed.

Lord Grey said: "Once you got fairly in and made it apparent to the whole world that you were making a serious effort to force the Straits, of course there was loss of prestige if you failed; but I do not think there would have been much lost if we had failed to take the outer forts and then gone away again."

Mr. Asquith stated: "One of the great reasons put forward in the first instance which appealed to Lord Kitchener and everybody was that if it was merely a naval attack, it could have been abandoned at any moment without any serious loss of prestige."

Mr. Arthur Balfour said: "I think it was always in the view of the Admiralty and of the responsible people that if the outer forts attack failed, you could always divert all your naval efforts to some other theatre of operations."

Sir Arthur Wilson, also, looking at the matter from the naval rather than from the political point of view, was asked the following question by Sir William Pickford: "So long as you were not so far committed that you could not stop, you did not see much objection to it?" His reply was: "I did not think there was any harm."

It will be seen in the sequel to this report that, when the time came for applying the principles enunciated above, the argument based upon the loss of prestige, which would result from the acknowledgment of a partial failure, exercised so predominant an influence as practically both to nullify the intentions which had been originally formed and to obliterate the recollection of the considerations which were advanced prior to any definite action having been taken.

The effect of modern artillery etc.

It may be as well here also to allude to another consideration which appears to have carried great weight at the War Council on the occasion of their meeting on January 28th. Sir Maurice Hankey gives the following amongst other reasons for differentiating the position in 1914–15 from that discussed by the Committee of Imperial Defence in 1907.

"The fall of the Liège and Namur forts had led to

the belief that permanent works were easily dealt with by modern long-range artillery, and this was confirmed by the fall of the outer forts.

The utilisation of aircraft had led to the hope that, in a comparatively confined space like the Gallipoli Peninsula, the value of naval bombardment, particularly by indirect laying, would be enormously increased."

We have received abundant evidence to show that these arguments weighed strongly both in the minds of Ministers and experts.

Lord Grey said: "The experience of this war was supposed to have changed the prospect of successful attack upon forts and made successful attack upon forts a practicable operation where it had not been a practicable operation before."

Mr. Churchill said: "This war had brought many surprises. We had seen fortresses reputed throughout Europe to be impregnable collapsing after a few days' attack by field armies without a regular siege."

The arguments involved in the consideration of this subject are of so highly technical a character that none but specialists can express any very confident opinion upon them. At the same time, the presumed analogy between the Belgian forts and the position in the Dardanelles weighed so strongly in the minds of the Government that we think it incumbent on us to deal briefly with the subject, and to state such conclusions as we have been able to form from the evidence laid before us.

It is, we think, correct to say that the rapid destruction of the Belgian fortresses by heavy howitzers came as a surprise in land warfare. It may be accounted for:—

1. By the foresight and reticence displayed by the German military authorities in ascertaining the results obtainable from the high-angle fire of howitzers of large calibre, and in providing the requisite ordnance and ammunition.
2. By the increased facilities now available for transporting and mounting such heavy ordnance.
3. By the advantage derivable from the use of aircraft for observing and reporting the fall of the projectiles.

It must also be remembered that, when the heavy armament of the fortresses had been dismounted or silenced, an ample military force was immediately forthcoming to seize and hold the works.

Comparing heavy howitzers as used in the destruction of the Antwerp, Namur and Liège forts with heavy guns, as mounted in the ships that made the attack on the Dardanelles, the advantages of the howitzer over the gun are:—

1. The projectile descends at such an obtuse angle that it clears the parapet or vertical defence of the guns in the forts and explodes more nearly in the centre and does more damage.
2. The penetration of any overhead protection of the forts is assured.

3. The steep angle of descent enables the projectiles to clear any hills in front of the forts and also to reach batteries in concealed positions, such as those mounted in a hollow of the land.

The disadvantages are:—

1. To ensure any degree of accuracy the howitzers must be fixed in relation to the object.
2. The wind, especially at very long ranges, is detrimental to the accuracy of fire.
3. The range is comparatively short.

The advantages of the gun over the howitzer are:—

1. Higher velocity and consequently greater penetration.
2. Greater accuracy.

The disadvantages are:—

1. Although penetration is greater, the protection that can be given to shore guns would probably resist all direct hits. There is no limit to the protection that may be given to guns in forts, and therefore to ensure each gun being silenced the gun itself would have to be hit.

    Guns as mounted on board ships cannot be given sufficient elevation to obtain high-angle fire similar to howitzers, but at long ranges or at short ranges by reducing the muzzle velocity an angle of descent of about 21 degrees can be obtained. The "Queen Elizabeth's" mountings can give about 20 degrees of elevation, but this is not sufficient for really high-angle fire. Thus, in the case of the "Queen Elizabeth", lying 15,000 yards from Gabe Tepe and firing with reduced three-quarter charge at Kilid Bahr, the angle of descent would be 17° 18'; firing at Chanak the angle of descent would be 20° 20'.

2. Guns, owing to the small angles of descent, are not able to attack concealed forts and batteries.

3. Guns mounted in ships cannot fire from concealed positions, but provided their gun power is greater than that of the forts, the ships could keep out of range.

Thus it will be seen that for the destruction of forts, and especially those in concealed positions, the howitzer is a superior weapon to the gun. With reference to Mr. Churchill's statement regarding the destruction of the Belgian fortresses, the new and surprising fact was mainly due to the causes we have mentioned, only the third of which is applicable to guns mounted on board ships. On the other hand, the improvement in the power of the latest naval guns in comparison with the defensive capabilities of forts is certainly appreciable, especially in the case of the heavy guns in the new ships—"Queen Elizabeth" and "Inflexible"—that were used in the Dardanelles operations.

In the case of the Dardanelles, the reduction of the forts was a very much more difficult and hazardous operation than the naval attacks which had failed in the cases of Port Arthur, Santiago or Wei-Hai-Wei, because after the outer forts were silenced, the forts on each side of a long, narrow strait had to be dealt with.

The waters readily lent themselves to be defended by mines, and the mine-fields could be easily protected by gun fire.

The facilities for firing Whitehead torpedoes from fixed tubes on each side of the Straits were very good, and many of these positions might be concealed. A certain number of them were known to exist.

The topography of the land on each side of the Straits was most favourable for concealed batteries of guns and howitzers, and the breadth of the Peninsula opposite Kilid Bahr was about 6 to 7 miles, and at Chanak was about 8 to 9 miles. Thus, ships bombarding those forts by indirect fire from off Gaba Tepe might find concealed batteries that would compel them to go some distance from the land, and might force them out of range. Ships bombarding from inside the Straits would also be fairly certain to be attacked by concealed batteries. Lastly, it was not certain when submarines might appear on the scene.

In the evidence of Mr. Churchill and certain naval officers of high position, stress was laid on the result of the bombardment of the outer forts as indicating what might be expected from similar action inside the Straits. In our opinion there was little analogy between the two operations, as in the former case the ships bombarding could keep out of range; the concealed batteries could not attack them; they were free from mines and Whitehead torpedoes.

The Fleet bombarding the Dardanelles had the important advantage over fleets previously engaged in the bombardment of forts that seaplanes were available for observation; but apparently they did not fulfil expectations, as the engine power was deficient, and there was much difficulty experienced in rising from the water when there was any sea.

In the bombardment of the outer forts ships were placed to observe the fall of the projectiles, and succeeded in doing so; but when the forts inside the Straits were attacked, ships were not very effective for this purpose, and it would seem that on the 18th March, when the determined attack was made, there was hardly any attempt to observe the fall of the shots.

Looking to all the facts of the case, we are disposed to think that undue importance was attached to the ease with which the Belgian forts were destroyed, and that the extent to which there was any analogy between those forts and the forts at the Dardanelles was over-rated.

The meeting of the War Council on January 28th

Mr. Churchill stated to us that, in the early days of January, Lord Fisher "assented" to the purely naval attack on the Dardanelles. It was, of course, known that, in common with all other experts, he would have preferred a joint naval and military attack had troops been available. It was also known that he would have preferred operations in another theatre of war. But, so far as we have been able to ascertain, there is no contemporary record to show that he expressed any opinion adverse to the proposed attack on the Dardanelles considered exclusively on its own merits.

Shortly after the meeting of January 13th, Lord Fisher's attitude underwent some change. The real divergence between his views and those of Mr. Churchill became more apparent than heretofore. The latter thus describes what occurred: "During the weeks that followed I could see that Lord Fisher was increasingly worried about the Dardanelles situation. He reproached himself for having agreed to begin the operation. Now it was going to broaden out into a far larger and far longer undertaking than he had contemplated, his great wish became to put a stop to the whole thing. Although our relations continued to be friendly and pleasant, it was clear to me that there was a change. Although we agreed on every definite practical step that had to be taken, there was a deep difference in our underlying view. He knew that I wanted the fleet to carry out its plan in its integrity. I knew that he wanted to break off the whole operation and come away."

Mr. Asquith has borne testimony to the fact that there were at this time constant differences of opinion between the First Lord and the First Sea Lord, but he added: "They got on well together, all the same." The evidence given to us by both Mr. Churchill and Lord Fisher amply confirms this latter statement.

These differences eventually culminated in the submission by Lord Fisher direct to the Prime Minister on January 25th of a Memorandum setting forth his views. It is an interesting and, in many respects, important paper. But it has no very direct bearing on the immediate subject of our inquiry. Moreover, inasmuch as it dwells exclusively on the general naval policy which should be adopted by this country, and does not discuss the practicability or otherwise of the attack on the Dardanelles, it would be most inadvisable that it should be reproduced in this report. It may, however, without detriment to the public interest, be said that Lord Fisher generally deprecated the use of the fleet for coastal bombardments or attacks on fortified positions. His Memorandum was immediately answered by another prepared by Mr. Churchill on January 27th, in which, whilst expressing full concurrence in the general principles of naval policy advocated by Lord Fisher, he contended that the proposal to bombard the Gallipoli Peninsula did not conflict with those principles. Mr. Churchill further informed us that it was not until he had seen Lord Fisher's Memorandum of January 26th, that he "perceived ... that the First Sea Lord had, since the first meeting of the War Council, developed serious misgivings about it" (*i.e.* about the decision taken on January 13th).

It appears that subsequent to the submission of this Memorandum, Lord Fisher intimated that he did not wish to attend any more meetings of the War Council. The Prime Minister was extremely desirous that Lord Fisher should not absent himself from the meeting which was about to take place. It was arranged, therefore, that, prior to the official meeting on January 28th,

Lord Fisher and Mr. Churchill should meet in the Prime Minister's room and discuss the matter with him. Save in respect to some points of slight importance as regards the precise language used, the accounts given to us by Mr Asquith and Lord Fisher, as regards what occurred at this private meeting, tally.

Mr. Churchill advocated the attack on the Dardanelles. Lord Fisher spoke in favour of those alternative schemes, which we have not thought it advisable to describe, but to which we have already alluded. He did not criticise the attack on the Gallipoli Peninsula on its own merits. Neither did he mention to the Prime Minister that he had any thought of resigning if his opinions were overruled. The Prime Minister, after hearing both sides, expressed his concurrence in Mr. Churchill's views. Immediately afterwards, the War Council met at 11.30 a.m.

Sir Maurice Hankey's record of this meeting, in so far as it concerns the subject of our inquiry, is as follows:—

"Mr. Churchill said that he had communicated to the Grand Duke Nicholas and to the French Admiralty the project for a naval attack on the Dardanelles. The Grand Duke had replied with enthusiasm, and believed that this might assist him. The French Admiralty had also sent a favourable reply, and had promised co-operation. Preparations were in hand for commencing about the middle of February. He asked if the War Council attached importance to this operation, which undoubtedly involved some risks.

Lord Fisher said that he had understood that this question would not be raised to-day. The Prime Minister was well aware of his own views in regard to it.

The Prime Minister said that, in view of the steps which had already been taken, the question could not well be left in abeyance.

Lord Kitchener considered the naval attack to be vitally important. If successful, its effect would be equivalent to that of a successful campaign fought with the new armies. One merit of the scheme was that, if satisfactory progress was not made, the attack could be broken off.

Mr. Balfour then dwelt on the advantages which would accrue from a successful attack on the Dardanelles, and concluded by saying that 'it was difficult to imagine a more helpful operation.'

Sir Edward Grey said it would also finally settle the attitude of Bulgaria and the whole of the Balkans.

Mr. Churchill said that the naval Commander-in-Chief of the Mediterranean had expressed his belief that it could be done. He required from three weeks to a month to accomplish it. The necessary ships were already on their way to the Dardanelles."

It is to be observed that the Memorandum addressed by Lord Fisher to the Prime Minister on January 25th was not in the hands of the War Council when this meeting took place, neither were they informed of the conversation between the Prime Minister, Lord Fisher and Mr. Churchill which immediately preceded the meeting. The result, coupled with Lord Fisher's silence, was that the Members of the War Council, although they may have had some rather vague idea that Lord Fisher was not in agreement with the First Lord, were by no means well-informed of his views.

Lord Fisher has explained to us the reasons of his silence. He "did not want to have an altercation with his Chief at the Council." Mr. Churchill, he said, "was my Chief, and it was silence or resignation." When asked what he meant by stating to the Council that "he had understood that the (Dardanelles) question would not be raised to-day," he replied: "I thought we would have time to think over it. I did not think that it would be gone on with at the meeting."

When Lord Fisher found that he was mistaken in this opinion and that a final decision was at once to be taken, he was greatly dissatisfied. He rose from his seat with the intention of going to the room of Mr. Bonham Carter, the Prime Minister's Private Secretary, and intimating his intention to resign. Lord Kitchener at the same time rose from his seat and, before Lord Fisher could leave the room, had some private conversation with him at the window. He strongly urged Lord Fisher not to resign, and pointed out that he was the only one present who disagreed with the Dardanelles operation. Eventually, according to a note Lord Fisher made at the time, the latter "reluctantly gave in to Lord Kitchener's entreaty and resumed his seat."

During all these proceedings, Sir Arthur Wilson, for reasons very analogous to those which inspired Lord Fisher's attitude, remained silent. In the course of his evidence he said to us that he was "moderately adverse" to the plan of bombarding the Dardanelles. He added: "I thought other things might be better, but both the First Lord and I recognised that it was not my business to interfere, and if they decided on a plan all I was to do was to help them to the best of my ability. In fact, the main object in my declining to have any official appointment was that I might be put into a position in which I should have to oppose the First Lord or the First Sea Lord, or to support one against the other."

The following extracts from Sir Arthur Wilson's evidence are also worthy of attention:

"*Admiral Sir William May.* In the discussions prior to the 13th January, leaving the First Lord out, was there any general consensus of opinion favourable to an exclusively naval attack?

A. I do not think there was.

Q. In representing the opinion of the Admiralty to the War Council on the 13th January or on the 28th January, did the First Lord reflect these unfavourable opinions?

A. No. I think he rather passed them over. He was very keen on his own views ...

Sir William Pickford. In what way did you think the First Lord on the 28th failed to represent the difficulties to the War Council?

A. In the first place, he kept on saying he could do it without the army; he only wanted the army to come in and reap the fruits, I think, was his expression; and I think he generally minimised the risks from mobile guns, and treated it as if the armoured ships were immune altogether from injury. I do not mean to say he actually said they were immune, but he minimised the risk a great deal."

Mr. Churchill, in answer to a question addressed to him by the Chairman, said:

"The effect produced upon my mind was that Sir Arthur Wilson's state of mind on the subject, which I watched very carefully, was favourable to the bombardment, and encouraged me in thinking the bombardment would be successful. All the same, if Sir Arthur Wilson had been asked to give a vote, he would have voted in the negative.

Q. He would have voted in the negative because he wanted to do some other operation?

A. Yes.

Q. He never said to you, on the ground of the merits of the thing itself and the practicability of the thing itself, independently of operations elsewhere, that he thought you had better not undertake that operation?

A. No one of those who were consulted—there were very few, but they were very important people—ever argued against the practicability. No one ever said: 'This is a thing which you

cannot do,' and showed by practical simple reasons that it could not be done; the only
arguments which were ever used were these general arguments which you have heard and I
thought myself to some extent a judge of those."

A further meeting took place on January 28th at
6 p. m., but in the interval between the two meetings
an incident occurred which is thus related by Mr.
Churchill: "Although the War Council had come to a
decision in which I heartily agreed, and no voice had
been raised against the naval plan, I felt I must come
to a clear understanding with the First Sea Lord. I had
noticed the incident of his leaving the table, and Lord
Kitchener following him to the window and arguing
with him, and I did not know what was the upshot in
his mind. After lunch I asked him to come to see me
in my room, and we had a talk. I strongly urged him
to undertake the operation, and he definitely consented to do so. I state this positively. We then repaired
to the afternoon War Council meeting, Admiral
Oliver, the Chief of the Staff, coming with us, and I
announced finally on behalf of the Admiralty and
with the agreement of Lord Fisher that we had
decided to undertake the task with which the War
Council had charged us so urgently.

"This I take as the point of final decision. After it,
I never looked back. We had left the region of discus-
sion and consultation, of balancings and misgivings.
The matter had passed into the domain of action."

Thus the third phase of these transactions was

reached. There was no longer, as on January 13th, any question of "preparing" for an attack on the Dardanelles. It was finally decided that an attack should be made, by the fleet alone, with Constantinople as its ultimate objective.

We wish to add some comments on these proceedings. Both Lord Fisher and Sir Arthur Wilson are distinguished officers who, in the course of their honourable careers, have rendered eminent services to their country. We have not the least doubt that the attitude which they adopted at the War Council was dictated by a strong sense of duty. But we have no hesitation in recording our opinion that it was a mistaken sense of duty. Lord Fisher, indeed, himself recognised that he "stretched loyalty to an extreme pitch."

It has probably happened to most officials who occupy or have occupied high places that they have at times disagreed with the heads of their departments. There may perhaps be occasions when such disagreement justifies resignation. But those occasions are extremely rare. More generally, it is the duty of the official not to resign but to state fully to the head of his department and, should any proper occasion arise, to other members of the Ministry, what are the nature of his views. Then, if after due consideration those views are over-ruled, he should do his best to carry out the policy of the Government, even although he may not be in personal agreement with it. This duty was in a very special degree incumbent upon an officer placed in Lord Fisher's position, though it perhaps applies to a somewhat less extent to Sir Arthur Wilson. Both of these officers were distinguished experts. They must have been aware that the questions which the Council had to decide were of so technical a nature that none but expert opinion could be of any value, and they must also have been aware that none of the Ministerial members of the Council had any expert naval knowledge.

We hold, therefore, that although they were not asked definitely to express their opinions, they should have done so. We dwell on this point because we consider that if the principles on which Lord Fisher and Sir Arthur Wilson acted were to be generally accepted by officials in other departments, they would exercise an extremely bad effect upon the general efficiency of the public services. They would tend to cripple independence of thought and their application would leave the Parliamentary heads of the various departments without that healthy assistance which they have a right to expect, and which is, at times, much more likely to be rendered by reasonable and deferential opposition than by mere agreement resting wholly on the ties of discipline.

There can be no doubt that at the two meetings on January 28th, Mr. Churchill strongly advocated the adoption of the Dardanelles enterprise. When Sir Arthur Wilson was asked "Did the First Lord express an opinion in favour of it?" he replied: "Yes; very much. He pressed it very strongly." We think that, considering what Mr. Churchill knew of the opinions entertained by Lord Fisher and Sir Arthur Wilson, and considering also the fact that the other experts at the Admiralty who had been consulted, although they assented to an attack on the outer forts of the Dardanelles and to progressive operations thereafter up the Straits as far as might be found practicable, had not done so with any great cordiality or enthusiasm, he ought, instead of urging Lord Fisher, as he seems to have done at the private meeting after luncheon on January 28th, to give a silent, but manifestly very reluctant, assent to the undertaking, not merely to have invited Lord Fisher and Sir Arthur Wilson to express their views freely to the Council, but further to have insisted on their doing so, in order that the Ministerial members might be placed in full possession of all the arguments for and against the enterprise. We have not the least doubt that, in speaking at the Council, Mr. Churchill thought that he was correctly representing the collective views of the Admiralty experts. But, without in any way wishing to impugn his good faith, it seems clear that he was carried away by his sanguine temperament and his firm belief in the success of the undertaking which he advocated. Although none of his expert advisers absolutely expressed dissent, all the evidence laid before us leads us to the conclusion that Mr. Churchill had obtained their support to a less extent than he himself imagined.

Further, we are very clearly of opinion that the other members of the Council, and more especially the Chairman, should have encouraged the experts present to give their opinion, and, indeed, should have insisted upon their doing so; and, moreover, that if the latter had expressed any doubts a short adjournment should have taken place, in order to allow the matter to be further considered, possibly by the light of what other experts, not having seats on the Council, might have to say. It was common knowledge that naval opinion generally condemned the attack on forts by ships unaided by any military force. The Prime Minister was himself aware of this fact. Such being the case, it would appear that special care should have been taken to elicit a full expression of the opinions entertained by the experts, and that they should have been urged to state them in their own way. What actually happened was that the stress laid upon the unquestionable advantages which would accrue from success was so great that the disadvantages which would arise in the not improbable case of failure were insufficiently considered.

∞∞◎∞∞

January 28th to February 16th

At the end of January the methods by which the Government hoped that the Fleet would reach Constantinople, if open to some objections on the ground of their practicability, were perfectly clear and comprehensible. They had resolved that an attempt should be made by the Fleet alone in order to force the passage of the Dardanelles. There was no intention of calling for military aid on any large scale. Admiral Carden thought that the operation was "worth trying," though at a later period, when he found that the defences "were much more extensive and powerful than had been anticipated," he changed his mind. In the first instance, he considered that only some small landing parties, consisting principally of Marines, would be required to complete the demolition of the forts. None of the responsible authorities appear to have paid much attention to the course of action which it would be necessary to adopt after the passage of the Dardanelles had been forced. Admiral Carden thought that "as the operations progressed he would receive further orders from the Admiralty as to the precise lines they wished him to act upon."

The fact that, even after the passage had been forced, communications with the Fleet in the Sea of Marmora might, to some extent, be impeded by such batteries as had not been destroyed, was recognised. But in London, where, according to General Callwell's evidence, the resistance likely to be offered by the Turks had, from the first, been greatly underestimated, no great importance appears to have been attached to this argument.

Lord Kitchener was of opinion that directly the passage had been forced the Gallipoli garrison would evacuate the Peninsula, inasmuch as their communications with Constantinople would be cut off. In a Memorandum dated March 23rd he wrote: "Once the ships are through, the position of the Gallipoli Peninsula ceases to be of any military importance." Moreover, he and others, including Lord Grey, confidently looked forward to a revolution taking place in Constantinople once the British Fleet appeared in the Sea of Marmora.

An officer from the Admiralty was asked the following question: "Did the intelligence in your possession favour the idea that the arrival of the British Fleet would have produced a revolution in Constantinople?" He replied: "Oh, yes; certainly it would. I feel no hesitation in saying that."

After the meeting of January 28th, the objective of the British Government remained the same, but the views entertained as to the means of realising it underwent a gradual but profound change. The necessity for employing a large military force became daily more apparent. The idea of a purely naval operation was gradually dropped. The prestige argument grew in importance. It does not appear that either the Cabinet or the War Council ever definitely discussed and deliberately changed the policy. General Callwell says that it would be very difficult to assign any date at which the change took place. "We drifted," he said, "into the big military attack."

At the evening meeting on January 28th, Lord Kitchener had stated very plainly, in connection with the question which was then under discussion of affording assistance to Serbia, that "we had at present no troops to spare." Mr. Churchill was of a different opinion. He said: "I assert that in February there was nothing in the situation in France, or on the Russian front, or in this island, which would have prevented the War Office from concentrating within striking distance either of

Salonika or the Dardanelles eight or nine, or even ten, infantry divisions." But, of course, on a matter of this sort Lord Kitchener's opinion carried the greatest weight. He would not go further than stating at a meeting which took place on February 9th that "if the Navy required the assistance of the land forces at a later stage, that assistance would be forthcoming."

There appears, indeed, to be some reason for supposing that Lord Kitchener realised from the first that the aid of the Army would eventually be necessary at the Dardanelles. At a meeting on May 14th, he said: "I realised that if the Fleet failed to achieve their object, the Army would have to be employed to help the Navy through."

On February 15th, Sir Henry Jackson wrote a long Memorandum, which was sent to Admiral Carden not as orders, but as "suggestions, to be adopted by him or not at his discretion."

This Memorandum concludes in the following terms:—

"The provision of the necessary military forces to enable the fruits of this heavy naval undertaking to be gathered must never be lost sight of; the transports carrying them should be in readiness to enter the Straits as soon as it is seen the forts at the Narrows will be silenced.

To complete their destruction, strong military landing parties with strong covering forces will be necessary. It is considered, however, that the full advantage of the undertaking would only be obtained by the occupation of the Peninsula by a military force acting in conjunction with the naval operations, as the pressure of a strong field army of the enemy on the Peninsula would not only greatly harass the operations, but would render the passage of the Straits impracticable by any but powerfully armed vessels, even though all the permanent defences had been silenced.

The naval bombardment is not recommended as a sound military operation, unless a strong military force is ready to assist in the operation, or, at least, follow it up immediately the forts are silenced."

A very important informal meeting of some of the Ministers took place on February 16th. It must be borne in mind that at that time no bombardment of the Gallipoli Peninsula had as yet taken place. The idea, therefore, of a purely naval operation was by no means abandoned. At the same time, owing to the repulse of the Turkish attack on Egypt, which had recently taken place, and to further changes in connection with plans in the Western theatre of war, to which we need not allude more particularly, it was decided to mass a considerable force in the Mediterranean to be used as occasion might require. Sir Maurice Hankey was, unfortunately, not present at this informal meeting, but the decisions which were arrived at were eventually incorporated into those of the War Council. They were as follows:—

1. The XXIXth Division, hitherto intended to form part of Sir John French's Army, to be despatched

to Lemnos at the earliest possible date. It is hoped that it may be able to sail within nine or ten days.

2. Arrangements to be made for a force to be despatched from Egypt, if required.

3. The whole of the above forces, in conjunction with the battalions of Royal Marines already despatched, to be available in case of necessity to support the naval attack on the Dardanelles.

4. Horse-boats to be taken out with the XXIXth Division, and the Admiralty to make arrangements to collect small craft, tugs, and lighters in the Levant.

5. The Admiralty to build special transports and lighters suitable for the conveyance and landing of a force of 50,000 men at any point where they may be required."

Sir Maurice Hankey states that this was "the all-important decision from which sprang the joint naval and military enterprise against the Gallipoli Peninsula." This decision may, in fact, be regarded as the fourth phase of the transactions. It had not been definitely decided to use troops on a large scale, but they were to be massed so as to be in readiness should their assistance be required.

‹oo✇oo›

The bombardment of February 19th

The first bombardment of the outer forts took place on February 19th. In his report on the operation, dated March 17th, Admiral Carden said: "The result of the day's action on the 19th February showed apparently that the effect of long-range bombardment by direct fire on modern earthwork forts is slight. Forts 1–4 appeared to be hit on many occasions by 12-inch common shell well placed; but when the ships closed in all four guns opened fire. And on the second day, although a heavy and prolonged fire at short range was poured into the forts, 70 per cent of the heavy guns were found to be in a serviceable condition when the demolition parties landed." In his evidence before us he qualified this by saying: "About 70 per cent. of the guns appeared to the officers in command of the landing parties to be efficient; but I do not think it actually follows that they were. Their magazines were all blown up; their electrical communications to their firing point or whatever their communications were, were probably all destroyed, so that though the gun itself was intact, it does not at all follow that it could be made effective under a considerable time . . . . The forts were in such a state when the bombardment was finished that it would have taken a considerable time to make use of even the guns that were not actually disabled by having the muzzles blown off or having a charge put in the breach or something of that sort; it would have taken a considerable time, I think, to make use of that 70 per cent. of guns. The personnel would have had to have been undisturbed for a considerable time to have come back to the forts and made use of that 70 per cent. of guns. But 70 per cent. of the guns were apparently intact on their mountings."

Vice-Admiral Sir Reginald Bacon, also, who can speak with authority on this subject, inasmuch as he has had, during the present war, a wide experience of bombardments in the North Sea, generally confirmed Admiral Carden's view. "If," he said, "they actually destroyed 30 per cent. in the short time they did very well."

It may here be mentioned that the decisions taken by the War Council on January 13th and 28th were not communicated to the whole of the Cabinet until a day or two before the bombardment took place. Mr. Asquith informed us that the approval of the Cabinet was "unanimous."

Mr. McKenna was the only Cabinet Minister who appeared before us and who was not present at the early meetings of the War Council. He was asked whether he concurred in the view that the Cabinet approved. His reply was as follows:—

"From Mr. Asquith's point of view I readily understand how he came to that conclusion. The statement was made to us that the War Council had come to a unanimous decision that the bombardment of the Dardanelles should be undertaken, and we were told that all the necessary orders had been given, and that the bombardment would open within either twenty-four or forty-eight hours of the time at which he was speaking. So far as my recollection goes, there was no comment and certainly no criticism of Mr. Asquith's statement, and consequently I do not think it was open to him to come to any other conclusion in the circumstances than that the Cabinet approved. But from my point of view and from the point of view of many of my colleagues with whom I have spoken on the subject, our view of the matter would be somewhat different. I should say for myself that I had not at the time the means of forming an opinion, much less of expressing one. We accepted without comment or criticism .... I fully recognise the justification for the Prime Minister in assuming our approval. Assent I distinguish from approval. He, having all the facts in his mind and not knowing how ignorant we were of the reasons which led up to it, assumed that assent was approval."

∘∘◦◆◇◆◦∘∘

February 16th to February 26th

Sir Maurice Hankey states in his Memorandum that
a series of "acute discussions" took place at the War
Council on February 19th, 24th and 26th.
Subsequent events proved that the decisions taken
during this period marked a very important epoch in
the first stage of the Dardanelles operations. It was in
the course of these ten days that the views of Lord
Kitchener, who was in reality the leading spirit of
the triumvirate which was conducting the war,

underwent a considerable change. It is not necessary to quote at length the proceedings which took place during this period, but it is essential to gain a clear insight into the nature and importance of the decisions which were actually taken.

The first point which must strike any one who has carefully studied the documents and listened to the evidence submitted to us is that the original idea of possibly breaking off the attack on the Dardanelles, which had manifestly been waning ever since its first conception early in January, altogether disappeared from the purview of the responsible authorities by the middle of February. At the meeting on the 24th, Lord Kitchener said that he "felt that if the Fleet would not get through the Straits unaided, the Army ought to see the business through. The effect of a defeat in the Orient would be very serious. There could be no going back. The publicity of the announcement had committed us." Lord Grey said that "failure would be morally equivalent to a great defeat on land." Whilst, however, the expression of these views is conclusive as showing that the original idea of limiting the operations wholly to the Fleet had been greatly modified, even if it had not been wholly abandoned, and that military operations on a large scale were contemplated, it is not easy to define with precision the nature of the programme which took its place. The scope of the intended military operations was left in doubt.

Lord Kitchener and others still clung to the idea that success was attainable by naval action alone. In the course of the discussion on February 24th he asked Mr. Churchill whether he "contemplated a land attack." The latter said, in reply, that "he did not, but it was quite conceivable that the naval attack might be temporarily held up by mines, and some local military operation required."

The telegrams sent from the War Office give some indication of what was passing in Lord Kitchener's mind at this time.

On February 23rd, he sent through Sir John Maxwell, who was in Egypt, instructions to General Birdwood, who was about to proceed to the Dardanelles, to report "whether it is considered by the Admiral that it will be necessary for troops to be employed to take the forts, and, if so, what force will be necessary; whether a landing force will be required of the troops to take the forts in reverse, and generally in what manner it is proposed to employ the troops."

On February 24th, he telegraphed to Sir John Maxwell: "It is proposed that the Navy should silence the guns and destroy the forts with gun fire. It is not intended that parties should be landed on the Gallipoli Peninsula, except under cover of the naval guns, to help in total demolition when the ships get to close quarters."

On February 26th, Sir John Maxwell telegraphed that the French officer, who had formerly been military attaché at Constantinople, thought that "a military expedition is essential for opening the Dardanelles passage to the Allied Fleet, and it would be extremely hazardous to land on the Gallipoli Peninsula, as the peninsula is very strongly organised for defence."

On the evening of the same day, Lord Kitchener telegraphed to General Birdwood through Sir John Maxwell: "The forcing of the Dardanelles is being undertaken by the Navy, and as far as can be foreseen at present the task of your troops, until such time as the passage has actually been secured, will be limited to minor operations, such as final destruction of batteries, after they have been silenced, under the covering fire of the battleships. It is possible, however, that howitzer batteries may be concealed inland with which the ships cannot deal effectively, and, if called upon by Admiral Carden, you might have to undertake special minor operations from within the Straits for dealing with these. Remember, however, that there are large enemy military forces stationed on both sides of the Straits, and you should not commit yourself to any enterprise of this class without aerial reconnaissance and assurance of ample covering fire by the Fleet. At any time during the bombardment of the Dardanelles you can, of course, apply for and obtain any additional forces from your corps in Egypt that you may require up to the total of its strength."

In the meanwhile, the Admiralty, in accordance with the decision arrived at on February 16th, had been preparing transports to convey the XXIXth Division to the Mediterranean. It was calculated that their departure would commence on the 22nd. On the 20th, however, Colonel Fitzgerald, Lord

Kitchener's Personal Military Secretary, called at the Admiralty and stated that it had been decided that the XXIXth Division were not to go.

This decision led to an acute difference of opinion between Lord Kitchener and Mr. Churchill. The discussions on the subject at the meetings of the War Council on February 24th and 26th were animated. Mr. Churchill made "the strongest possible appeal" for the immediate despatch of the XXIXth Division. He formally recorded his dissent at the Division being retained in this country, and added that he "must disclaim all responsibility if disaster occurred in Turkey owing to the insufficiency of troops." Lord Kitchener, on the other hand, held that the Naval Division and Marines, together with the Australians and New Zealanders, whom it was proposed to bring from Egypt, constituted an adequate force and that the 33,000 men available from the XXIXth Division and a Territorial Division which it was proposed to send from home would not be likely to make the difference between success and failure. He was also uneasy about the position both in the Western and Russian theatres of war. He therefore declined to yield, and the Council, although Mr. Churchill's views appear to have received some support, finally decided in accordance with Lord Kitchener's advice.

It is clear that, at the time of the discussion, Lord Kitchener still thought that the Fleet, unaided, would be able to obtain entrance into the Sea of Marmora. "He felt convinced, from his knowledge of Constantinople and the East, that the whole situation in Constantinople would change the moment the Fleet had secured a passage through the Dardanelles. We should be in a better position to judge the situation when the defences at the Narrows began to collapse."

With the decision finally taken on February 26th, the fifth phase in these transactions may be said to have closed. On February 16th, it had been decided to employ troops on a large scale. This decision still held good, but its execution was to be delayed. At the same time, the idea of forcing the Dardanelles by the action of the Fleet alone had not been abandoned.

∞∞∞∞∞

February 26th to March 10th

Another meeting of the War Council was held on March 3rd. By this time Lord Kitchener's opposition to the despatch of the XXIXth Division had apparently weakened. On the question being raised by Mr. Churchill, he said that "he proposed to leave the question open until March 10th, when he hoped to have heard from General Birdwood."

General Birdwood, however, arrived at the Dardanelles before the 10th. On the 5th, he telegraphed to Lord Kitchener: "I am very doubtful if the Navy can force the passage unassisted. In any event the forcing of the passage must take a considerable time; the forts that have been taken up to the present have been visible and very easy, as the ships could stand off and shoot from anywhere, but inside the Straits the ships are bothered by unknown fire."

This was followed on the 6th by a telegram to the following effect: "I have already informed you that I consider the Admiral's forecast is too sanguine, and though we may have a better estimate by March 12th, I doubt his ability to force the passage unaided." On March 10th, Lord Kitchener, being then somewhat reassured as regards the position in other theatres of war, and being also possibly impressed by General Birdwood's reports, announced to the War Council that "he felt that the situation was now sufficiently secure to justify the despatch of the XXIXth Division."

The sixth phase in these transactions was thus reached. The decision of February 16th, the execution of which had been suspended on the 20th, again became operative on March 10th. In the meanwhile, three weeks of valuable time had been lost. The transports, which might have left on February 22nd, did not get away till March 16th.

It is with great reluctance and hesitation that we comment on these proceedings, for it is obvious that Lord Kitchener was mainly responsible for the decisions taken during the critical period between February 16th and March 10th, and it is quite possible that, were he alive, he might be able to throw a new light upon them. Nevertheless, we think it is incumbent on us to state the conclusions at which, with the evidence before us, we have arrived.

Lord Kitchener's position at this time was one of great difficulty. With the forces at his disposal he had to provide for home defence and also for maintaining an adequate force both in Flanders and Egypt. Was he to add to the demands which he had to meet the further liability of undertaking an additional military operation on a large scale in another and distant theatre of war? It can be no matter for surprise that he hesitated to do so. Subsequent events showed that the fears he entertained for the immediate future were groundless, but to impute any shadow of blame on that account would involve judging by the light of the wisdom which is the product of after-knowledge. Dealing, however, solely with the evidence which was available at the time, it certainly seems strange that the actualities of the situation should not have been more fully realised both by Lord Kitchener and his colleagues.

From the moment when large bodies of troops were massed in the immediate neighbourhood of the Dardanelles, even although they were not landed, the situation underwent a material change. Whatever may have been the intentions of the Government, the public opinion of the world must have been led to believe that an intention existed of making a serious attack both by land and sea. The loss-of-prestige argument, therefore, naturally acquired greater force than had been formerly the case. From the time the decision of February 16th was taken there were really only two alternatives which were thoroughly defensible.

One was to accept the view that by reason of our existing commitments elsewhere an adequate force could not be made available for expeditionary action in the Eastern Mediterranean; to face the possible loss of prestige which would have been involved in an acknowledgment of partial failure, and to have fallen back on the original plan of abandoning the naval attack on the Dardanelles, when once it became apparent that military operations on a large scale would be necessary.

The other was to have boldly faced the risks which would have been involved elsewhere and at once to have made a determined effort to force the passage of the Dardanelles by a rapid and well-organised combined attack in great strength. Unfortunately, the Government adopted neither of these courses. Time, as Mr. Asquith very truly said to us, was all-important. Yet for at least three weeks the Government vacillated and came to no definite decision in one sense or the other.

The natural result ensued. The favourable moment for action was allowed to lapse. Time was given to the Turks, with the help of German officers, to strengthen their position, so that eventually the opposition to be encountered became of a far more formidable character than was originally to have been anticipated. Moreover, even when the decision was taken, it was by no means thorough.

As we shall presently show, the hope of dispensing altogether with military assistance, save in respect to what were called "minor operations," was not abandoned. We think that Mr. Churchill was quite justified in attaching the utmost importance to the delays which occurred in despatching the XXIXth Division and the Territorial Division from this country.

Appointment of General Sir Ian Hamilton

Early in March it was decided to send out General Sir
Ian Hamilton to command the troops which were
being assembled in the neighbourhood of the
Dardanelles. His instructions are dated March 13th.
These and the conversation he had with Lord
Kitchener immediately before his departure from
London render it abundantly clear that the scope of
the intended military operations was at that time not
fully decided. Sir Ian Hamilton's instructions contain
the following passages:—

1. The Fleet have undertaken to force the passage of the Dardanelles. The employment of military forces on any large scale for land operations at this juncture is only contemplated in the event of the Fleet failing to get through after every effort has been exhausted.

2. Before any serious undertaking is carried out in the Gallipoli Peninsula, all the British military forces detailed for the expedition should be assembled, so that their full weight can be thrown in.

3. Having entered on the project of forcing the Straits, there can be no idea of abandoning the scheme. It will require time, patience and methodical plans of co-operation between the naval and military commanders. The essential point is to avoid a check which will jeopardise our chances of strategical and political success.

4. This does not preclude the probability of minor operations being engaged upon to clear areas occupied by the Turks with guns annoying the Fleet or for the demolition of forts already silenced by the Fleet. But such minor operations should be as much as possible restricted to the forces necessary to achieve the object in view, and should as far as practicable not entail permanent occupation of positions on the Gallipoli Peninsula.

Sir Ian Hamilton, in the evidence which he gave before us, dwelt strongly on the total absence of information furnished to him by the War Office Staff. No preliminary scheme of operations had been drawn up. "The Army Council had disappeared." No arrangements had been made about water supply. There was "a great want of staff preparation."

As regards the verbal instructions given to him by Lord Kitchener before he left London, he spoke as follows:—

"*Mr. Roch*: Did you gather from that conversation with Lord Kitchener that he contemplated military operations then?

A. No; he repeatedly said—he broke in talking about landing by saying: 'I do not expect you to do it at all. I hope to get through without it.' He contemplated certainly landing on the Bosphorus.

Q. As far as I gather he contemplated that the Navy would do the forcing of the Straits?

A. Certainly.

Q. And you went out under that impression?

A. Yes, I did entirely.

Q. Until you got the telegram from Lord Kitchener of the 19th March those were the first instructions you received from him that you were to undertake landing operations to take the Peninsula?

A. No doubt in conversation with me Lord Kitchener did contemplate such a thing, except that he insisted I must not do so piecemeal.

Q. You recollect the telegram: 'You know my views that the passage of the Dardanelles must be forced,' and so on—'those operations must be undertaken after careful consideration.' I read those as rather peremptory instructions that you were to take the Peninsula?

A. Undoubtedly.

Q. That is how I read it, and that is the way you read it?

A. Yes. I do not mean to say I had altogether parted with my discretion, and if I had chosen to say, 'This is altogether an impossibility,' I might have said so, but I did not think so."

∘∘◇✕◇∘∘

March 10th to March 16th

Between March 10th and March 16th some impor-
tant telegrams were exchanged between the First
Lord and Admiral Carden. On March 11th, the First
Lord sent the following telegram to the Admiral:—

"[101] Personal and Secret. Caution and deliberate methods were emphasised in your original
instructions, and the skill and patience which has
enabled your progress to be carried thus far without
loss are highly appreciated.

"If, however, success cannot be obtained without loss of ships and men, results to be gained are important enough to justify such a loss. The whole operation may be decided and consequences of a decisive character upon the war may be produced by the turning of the corner Chanak; and we suggest for your consideration that a point has now been reached when it is necessary to choose favourable weather conditions to over-whelm forts of the Narrows at decisive range by bringing to bear upon them the fire of the largest possible number of guns, great and small. Under cover of this fire landing parties might destroy the guns of the forts, and sweeping operations to clear as much as possible of the mine-field might also be carried out.

"It might be necessary to repeat the operation until the destruction of all the forts at the Narrows and the clearing of the approaches of mines had been accomplished.

"We have no wish to hurry you or urge you beyond your judgment, but we recognise clearly that at a certain period in your operations you will have to press hard for a decision; and we desire to know whether, in your opinion, that period has now arrived. Every well-conceived action for forcing a decision, even should regrettable losses be entailed, will receive our support.

"Before you take any decisive departure from the present policy we wish to hear your views."

At midnight on March 13th, Admiral Carden replied:—

"Your 101 is fully concurred in by me.

"I consider the stage when vigorous sustained action is necessary for success has now been reached. I am of opinion that, in order to ensure my communication line immediately Fleet enters the Sea of Marmora, military operations on a large scale should be opened at once."

On March 15th, the First Lord sent the following further telegram to Admiral Carden:

"[109] When General Hamilton arrives on Tuesday night concert with him in any military operations on large scale which you consider necessary ... The XXIXth Division (18,000 additional men) cannot arrive till the 2nd April.

"We understand that a good clear passage is intended to be swept through the minefields, and the forts at the Narrows eventually attacked at close range. Further, that the battle fleet will support by its fire as necessary the operations against the forts or the light and movable armament, and that several days will be required to complete this task. We understand that you propose then to put the forts at the Narrows effectually out of action by engaging them at a decisive range, and that when this is done forts beyond will be attacked at convenience, and further sweeping carried out as necessary. Assuming this to be your intention, we cordially approve it and desire the scheme to be pressed forward. No time is to be lost, but there should be no undue haste. We gather that an attempt to rush the passage without having previously cleared a channel through the mines and destroyed the primary armament of the forts is not contemplated at this stage. No operation of this nature should be decided upon before consulting us. Before undertaking it careful study will be required of the parts to be played by the Army and Navy in close co-operation, and it might then be found that a naval rush will be costly, without decisive military action to take the Kilid Bahr plateau."

On March 16th, Admiral Carden replied:—

"Your 109. I will consult with General Hamilton as soon as he arrives. My intentions are exactly expressed by your second paragraph. Plans of operations are practically complete, and I hope to commence on the 17th March; but as it is essential to have good visibility and a wind which will prevent smoke interference, a later date may be chosen. Meanwhile, careful search is being made for mines in the area in which ships will have to manoeuvre ...

"It is not intended to rush the passage before a channel is cleared."

On March 16th, Admiral Carden was obliged to resign his command for reasons wholly based on the state of his health.

The appointment of Admiral de Robeck

On March 17th, the First Lord sent the following telegram to Vice-Admiral de Robeck:

"Secret and Personal. I am conferring upon you the command of the Mediterranean Detached Fleet, with fullest confidence in your ability. In doing so I presume that you fully agree with Admiralty telegrams 101 and 109 and your predecessor's replies thereto, and that in your independent and separate judgment the immediate operations proposed are practicable. Do not hesitate to say if you think otherwise. If you agree, the operations should be carried out without delay and without further reference at the first favourable opportunity. You should work in closest harmony with General Hamilton."

On the same day (March 17th) Admiral de Robeck replied:—

"[105] Personal and Secret. I am very grateful for your telegram. Telegrams mentioned by you meet with my full concurrence.

"Weather permitting, I will proceed with operations to-morrow.

"I am convinced that success depends on our ability to clear the mine-fields for forcing Narrows. To do this successfully the forts must be silenced while sweeping operations are in progress.

"I have had to-day an entirely satisfactory interview with Generals Hamilton and D'Amade and Admiral Wemyss on my flagship."

The following extracts from Admiral de Robeck's evidence give some indication of the manner in which at the time he approached the subject:—

"*The Chairman.* Did you agree that that operation (*i.e.*, the destruction of the forts without military aid) was practicable?

A. I think everyone thought it was better to have a combined operation, but one was not consulted as to whether it was the right way to do it or not—we were told to bombard these forts, so we did it.

Q. You were told from the Admiralty?

A. Yes.

Q. Was that your view of what Admiral Carden thought—that he was told to do it—that he had no discretion?

A. I think he was directly told to get on and do it.

Q. Therefore, you were in agreement with Admiral Carden as to the possibility of a success-ful issue to the operations which were then being proposed?

A. Yes.

Q. That is to say, that you thought the forts could be demolished one by one without the help of an army?

A. Well, you see, I say that depended on clearing the mine-field. You see I add: 'It depends on our ability to clear the mine-field in forcing the Narrows.' That is telegram 105.

Q. When you got the telegram from the Admiralty did you consider that there was any sort of moral pressure being put on you to agree, or that you were free to give an independent judgment?

A. I think I would always give my opinion. Of course, one thing one must remember—at that time we had already started the operation. We had already bombarded the outer forts once, so that the operation had begun. In my opinion it would never have done then to have stopped at that moment, having once commenced the attack.

Q. It would never have done on what ground?

A. I think as regards the Turks.

Q. On purely naval or on political grounds?

A. On political grounds, I think; not on naval grounds.

Q. You thought there would be very great loss of prestige if we had stopped then?

A. Yes ...

Mr. Fisher ....

A. What was in our minds was that we would have got straight through to Constantinople, and it was generally anticipated that the arrival of the Fleet there would be the end of the ruling powers in Turkey. That was what we were always given to understand—that there would have been a revolution in Constantinople if we had arrived there with the Fleet ...

Sir Frederick Cawley. As a matter of fact, you entirely relied upon the political situation—that there would be a revolution in Turkey and that the whole situation would be altered, so that you would not need supplies, and you would not need a force to make good your position?

A. We fully realised that we could only stay in the Marmora, if they did not alter their attitude, for a given length of time, say a fortnight, or at the most three weeks.

Q. If you had got through, transports could not have followed you up?

A. Then, I think not—not with the guns we could not get at.

Q. And if this political situation had not so changed to our advantage, and there had not been a revolution, our Fleet would have been bottled up there?

A. We should have had to come down again. Yes, like Admiral Duckworth ...

Mr. Clyde. What ground had you then on the 17th of March for concurrence?

A. The necessity for going on. We were sent there to carry out a certain object, and the thing was to try and do it.

Q. I think from the first when you went there you rather looked at the matter from the point of view of an Admiralty order to force the Dardanelles, and your job was to do it if you could?

A. Yes; that was our first object. Therefore, the order was to carry out a certain operation or try and do it, and we had to do the best we could."

From these explanations it may be gathered that Admiral de Robeck at the time considered the exclusively naval operation practicable if only the mine-field could be cleared, that his opinion was greatly influenced by political considerations, and particularly by the loss of prestige which would be involved if the attack were abandoned, and that the main reason which dictated the answer sent to the Admiralty questions on March 17th was "the necessity of going on." In fact, Admiral De Robeck thought he had orders to force the passage of the Dardanelles, and that it was his duty to do his best to carry out those orders.

The bombardment of March 18th

The facts connected with the bombardment on March 18th are already so well known that we need not dwell on them at any length. The results may be summarised as follows:—

The "Irresistible," the "Ocean" and the "Bouvet" were sunk, and the crew of the latter were nearly all lost.

Admiral de Robeck reported: "Squadron is ready for immediate action except as regards ships lost and damaged, but it is necessary to reconsider the plan of attack. A method of dealing with floating mines must be found."

⊷⊷⊶⊷⊷

Events from March 19th to March 23rd

On March 19th, Sir Ian Hamilton telegraphed to Lord Kitchener: "I have not yet received any report on the naval action, but from what I actually saw of the extraordinarily gallant attempt made yesterday I am being most reluctantly driven towards the conclusion that the Dardanelles are less likely to be forced by battleships than at one time seemed probable, and that if the Army is to participate its operations will not assume the subsidiary form anticipated.

"The Army's share will not be a case of landing parties for the destruction of forts, etc., but rather a case of a deliberate and progressive military operation carried out in force in order to make good the passage of the Navy."

Lord Kitchener at once replied in the following terms: "You know my views that the passage of the Dardanelles must be forced, and that if large military operations on the Gallipoli Peninsula by the Army are necessary to clear the way, those operations must be undertaken after careful consideration of the local defences, and must be carried through." We have already mentioned that Sir Ian Hamilton regarded this telegram in the light of a "peremptory instruction that he was to take the Peninsula." We think that he was justified in doing so.

On March 22nd, Sir Ian Hamilton again telegraphed to Lord Kitchener stating that he proposed to go to Alexandria. On March 23rd, Lord Kitchener telegraphed to Sir Ian Hamilton: "I hear that April 14th is considered by you as about the date for commencement of military operations if the Dardanelles have not been forced by the Fleet before that date. I think that you had better know at once that I regard any such postponement as far too long. I should like to know how soon you could act on shore."

These telegrams are conclusive proof that Lord Kitchener had by that time wholly abandoned the idea of a purely naval operation, and realised the fact that military operations on a large scale were necessary. The telegrams also prove that Lord Kitchener, in contemplating military action, had no clear idea as to when a landing could be made. As a matter of fact the landing did not take place until April 25th.

On March 23rd, Sir Ian Hamilton telegraphed to Lord Kitchener: "I have now conferred with Admiral and we are equally convinced that to enable the Fleet effectively to force the passage of the Dardanelles the co-operation of the whole military force will be necessary."

The first impression produced by the receipt of the news of the bombardment was that the naval operations should continue in spite of the losses which had been incurred. The following statement in Mr. Churchill's narrative shows what happened. "I regarded it as only the first of several days' fighting, though the loss in ships sunk or disabled was unpleasant. It never occurred to me for a moment that we should not go on, within the limits of what we had decided to risk, till we reached a decision one way or the other. I found Lord Fisher and Sir Arthur Wilson in the same mood. Both met me that morning (the 19th) with expressions of firm determination to fight it out. The First Sea Lord immediately ordered two battleships, 'London' and 'Prince of Wales,' to reinforce Admiral de Robeck's fleet to replace casualties, in addition to the 'Queen' and 'Implacable,' which were on the way."

It should also be added that the French Ministry of Marine ordered another old battleship, the "Henri IV," to replace the "Bouvet" which had been lost. The first telegrams received from Admiral de Robeck dated March 19th and 20th clearly indicate that he shared the view entertained at the Admiralty. On the latter date, especially, he said: "Dardanelles will not be entered by any ships unless everything is ready for sustained attack. Meantime, in order to draw off some of enemy's field guns, feints at landing in various places will be made."

A meeting of the War Council was held on the morning of the 19th, at which it was decided "to inform Vice-Admiral de Robeck that he could continue the naval operation against the Dardanelles if he thought fit."

On March 23rd, however, Admiral de Robeck changed his views. He spoke of the "mine menace" being "much greater than we expected." He said that time would be required for "careful and thorough treatment, both in respect of mines and floating mines." He added: "Time will be required for this, but arrangements can be made by the time the army will be ready. A decisive operation about the middle of next month appears to me better than to take great risks for what may well be only half measures." He further said: "It does not appear to me practicable to land a sufficient force inside the Dardanelles to carry out this service. This view is shared by General Hamilton."

On the 26th, Admiral de Robeck further telegraphed: "The check on the 18th March is not, in my opinion, decisive, but on the 22nd March I met General Hamilton and heard his views, and I now think that, to obtain important results and to achieve the object of the campaign, a combined operation will be essential."

This telegram, Mr. Churchill says, "involved a complete change of plan and was a vital decision. I regretted it very much. I believed then, as I believe now, that we were separated by very little from complete success."

The whole question was then discussed at great length at the Admiralty. Mr. Churchill records: "I proposed that we should direct the Admiral to renew the naval attack, according to his previous intention. The First Sea Lord, however, did not agree; nor did Sir Arthur Wilson; nor did Sir Henry Jackson. Lord Fisher took the line that hitherto he had been willing to carry the enterprise forward, because it was supported and recommended by the Commander on the spot. But now that Admiral de Robeck and Sir Ian Hamilton had decided upon a joint operation, we were bound to accept their view.

"I do not at all blame Lord Fisher for this decision. The arguments for it were very strong indeed. But so were the arguments against it. Both the Prime Minister and Mr. Balfour, with whom I discussed the matter, were inclined to my view, but as our professional advisers and the Admiral on the spot were against it, it was impossible to go further, and I bowed to their decision. But with regret and anxiety."

This was the last phase of the "origin and inception" period. From this time onward two points became perfectly clear. One was that the Government had no intention of abandoning the attack on the Dardanelles; the second was that the attack would be made both by the Navy and by military forces who would be employed on a large scale.

The various stages through which these transactions passed may be summarised as follows:—

1. As early as November, 1914, the idea of attacking the Dardanelles had been mooted, but there does not appear at that time to have been any sort of intention of making a purely naval attack.

2. On January 3rd, 1915, the Russian Government were informed that a "demonstration" would be made against the Turks in some quarter.

3. On January 13th, the Admiralty were instructed to "prepare" for an attack on the Dardanelles. It was understood at the time by the First Lord, and apparently by others, that this involved approval of the attack. The intention at the time was that the operations should be purely naval and that no troops, save small parties for such purposes as the demolition of forts, should be used. It was thought that if the experience gained by attacking the outer forts was unsatisfactory, the attack might be broken off without any loss of prestige.

4. On January 28th, the decision to attack the Dardanelles by ships alone was definitely confirmed. There was still no intention of using troops, save for minor operations.

5. On February 16th, it was decided to mass large

bodies of troops in the neighbourhood of the Dardanelles with a view to assisting further operations when once the Fleet had forced a passage.

6. On February 19th, the first bombardment took place. The results were not decisive, but at the same time were fairly satisfactory.

7. On February 20th, principally owing to the anxiety felt by Lord Kitchener in respect to the state of affairs in other theatres of war, the decision to send troops from England to the Dardanelles was suspended.

8. On March 10th, Lord Kitchener resolved to sanction the departure of troops from England.

9. On March 18th, the second bombardment took place. The losses incurred were heavy, but, in the first instance, both Admiral de Robeck and the officials at the Admiralty wished to continue the purely naval attack.

10. On March 23rd, owing to representations made by Admiral de Robeck and Sir Ian Hamilton, it was decided to postpone further operations until adequate military forces could be assembled. The idea of making a purely naval attack was definitely abandoned.

There can be no doubt that, as a result of these and subsequent operations the main objective, as defined in the decision of the War Council on January 13th, was not attained. The attempt to force the Dardanelles and to reach Constantinople failed.

It would, however, be an exaggeration to say that the expedition, considered as a whole, was a complete failure. Such was by no means the case. The enterprise was originally undertaken in order to create a diversion in favour of the Russians. In this respect it may be said to have been very fairly successful.

Another point to which great importance was attached was to influence the attitude of all the Balkan States, and especially to secure the neutrality of Bulgaria. That neutrality was not secured, but it can scarcely be doubted that, had it not been for the Dardanelles expedition, Bulgaria would have joined the Central Powers at a far earlier date than was actually the case. Further, a large force of Turks, which might have been employed in other theatres of war, was for some long while immobilised.

The Prime Minister spoke very decisively on these points. We give the following extracts from his evidence:—

"*The Chairman*. In spite of the fact that it was a failure in one sense, do you think it was a success in another, and that if you had not carried out that expedition to the Dardanelles, the position of the Allies would have been very much worse than it is now?

A. Yes, I am unhesitatingly of that opinion. I say so now, after all the experience we have gained, and after what one must admit to have been the ultimate failure of the expedition. I say deliberately that there is no operation in the whole of this war which promised better results than the

Dardanelles operation. If it had succeeded, and it would have succeeded but for things which in the course of your enquiry you will come across and no doubt pronounce upon, in my judgment it would have produced a far greater effect upon the whole conduct of the war than anything that has been done in any other sphere of the war.

Q. I think nobody can doubt that for a moment, but it does not go very far. If successful it would have had an enormous effect; but the question I wanted to ask you was this; even as it was, you think the effect was very beneficial?

A. I do, even though it failed. If you like I will tell you why.

Q. Yes, please.

A. I will give you two reasons. There are a great many I might give, but I will give two. In the first place, it undoubtedly staved off and postponed for months the adhesion of Bulgaria to the Central Powers. There is no doubt whatever about that. In the second place—and this was the point Lord Kitchener always insisted upon up to the end—he said to me a hundred times it contained and immobilised very nearly 300,000 Turkish soldiers for the best part of nine months, who otherwise would have been a most formidable accretion to the enemy forces. Even though it failed, I consider it had very effective and powerful results.

Q. You feel very confident that the Bulgarians would have gone in on the German side sooner if it had not been for that?

A. Yes, I am certain of it."

Lord Grey also said:

"I have no doubt whatever that some untoward
consequence would have happened if it had not
been for the Dardanelles operations. Whether the
staving off of those untoward consequences was
worth the cost of life and the expenditure of
energy, ending of course in failure to get through,
is a matter really on which everyone must form
their own opinion. I can only state that there
were certain consequences which would have
happened sooner if the Dardanelles Expedition
had not been going on. I should strongly contro-
vert any statement that the expedition was of no
use at all.

Q. You think it was decidedly of use?

A. Yes, I think it was decidedly of use; but if you
put the question whether it was worth such a
tremendous expenditure of effort, that must
remain a matter of opinion.

Q. But it did gain valuable time?

A. It did gain valuable time.

Q. And heartened the Russians?

A. Oh, yes, it did."

We are generally in agreement with these views
expressed by Mr. Asquith and Lord Grey, but we
regard Lord Kitchener's estimate of the number of

Turkish troops immobilised for nearly nine months as conjectural.

Whether the advantages obtained were in any degree commensurate with the loss of valuable lives and treasure which was incurred, must, of course, as Lord Grey very truly said, remain a matter of opinion, but there can be no doubt that those advantages were important.

We repeat that it would be an exaggeration to regard the Dardanelles Expedition as a complete failure. We have already mentioned that the loss of prestige in abandoning the expedition, which at one time caused great anxiety, was in reality inappreciable.

It is interesting, but perhaps not very profitable, to speculate on what might have occurred if, subsequent to the bombardment of March 18th, the naval attack had been at once pressed on aided by such troops as were then on the spot. We have already stated that Mr. Churchill was strongly in favour of adopting this course, and that he received some support both from Mr. Asquith and Mr. Balfour. The idea, however, had to be abandoned because the weight of both naval and military authority was much opposed to it. But there were exceptions. Commodore de Bartolomé agreed with Mr. Churchill. Sir Ian Hamilton also stated that General Birdwood wished to "land at once," and he added "I think there was a good deal to be said for it." Sir Ian, however, held that "Lord Kitchener's original orders not to land if he could avoid it" held good.

Enver Pasha, at a much later date, is reported to

have said: "If the English had only the courage to rush more ships through the Dardanelles they could have got to Constantinople, but their delay enabled us thoroughly to fortify the Peninsula, and in six weeks' time we had taken down there over 200 Austrian Skoda guns."

At the time of the bombardment it was suspected by the Admiralty that the forts of the Dardanelles were getting short of ammunition. Evidence was subsequently obtained which showed that the suspicion was well-grounded.

Mr. Asquith, in dealing with this branch of the question, said: "I have always thought myself—but it is an opinion of no value, because it is the opinion of a layman—that if they had pushed then they would have got through, in which case the results would have been incalculable."

Whatever weight may be attached to these opinions and reports it must be remembered that out of the sixteen ships which attacked the Straits on March 18th, three were sunk and four were rendered unfit for further immediate action. Had the attack been renewed within a day or two there is no reason to suppose that the proportion of casualties would have been less, and, if so, even had the second attack succeeded, a very weak force would have been left for subsequent naval operations.

Conclusions

We trust that we have given so full a summary of the somewhat involved events, which have formed the subject of our enquiry, that any member of the public who reads this report will be able to draw his own conclusions. Those conclusions, it may be anticipated with some confidence, will vary.

The facts, indeed, are such that no one, who approaches the subject in a thoroughly judicial spirit, will be inclined to dogmatise about them. Notably, there is wide room for difference of opinion as to the relative degree of responsibility, as also to the amount of praise or blame which may reasonably be assigned to the principal authorities and departments concerned. All we can say is that we have endeavoured to the best of our ability to assess this responsibility, judging wholly by the evidence which has been laid before us to the complete exclusion of all other considerations of whatsoever character. It is for others to judge how far we have succeeded in this attempt.

The general conclusions at which we have arrived are as follows:—

(a) The question of attacking the Dardanelles was, on the initiation of Mr. Churchill, brought under the consideration of the War Council, on November 25th, 1914, as "the ideal method" for defending Egypt.

(b) It may reasonably be assumed that, inasmuch as all the authorities concerned were, *prima facie*, in favour of a joint naval and military rather than a purely naval attack, such attack, if undertaken at all, would have been of the former rather than of the latter character had not other circumstances led to a modification of the programme.

(c) The communication from the Russian Government on January 2nd introduced a fresh element into the case. The British Government considered that something must be done in response to it, and in this connection the question

of attacking the Dardanelles was again raised. The
Secretary of State for War declared that there were
no troops immediately available for operations in
the East. This statement was accepted by the War
Council, who took no steps to satisfy themselves
by reports or estimates as to what troops were
available then or in the near future. Had this been
done we think that it would have been ascertained
that sufficient troops would have been available
for a joint naval and military operation at an
earlier date than was supposed. But this matter was
not adequately investigated by the War Council.
Thus the question before the War Council on
January 13th was whether no action of any kind
should, for the time being, be undertaken, or
whether action should be taken by the Fleet
alone, the navy being held to be the only force
available.

(d) The political arguments which were adduced to
the War Council in favour of prompt and
effective action, if such were practicable, were
valid and of the highest importance, but the
practicability of whatever action was proposed
was of equal importance.

(e) Mr. Churchill appears to have advocated the
attack by ships alone before the War Council on
a certain amount of half-hearted and hesitating
expert opinion, which favoured a tentative or
progressive scheme, beginning with an attack
upon the outer forts. This attack, if successful,
was to be followed by further operations against

the main defences of the Narrows. There does not appear to have been direct support or direct opposition from the responsible naval and military advisers, Lord Fisher and Sir James Wolfe Murray, as to the practicability of carrying on the operation as approved by the War Council, viz., "To bombard and take the Gallipoli Peninsula, with Constantinople as its objective."

(f) The First Sea Lord and Sir Arthur Wilson, who was the only other Naval Adviser present at the War Council, expressed no dissent. Lord Kitchener, who occupied a commanding position at the time the decision was taken, was in favour of the project. Both Lord Fisher and Sir Arthur Wilson would have preferred a joint naval and military attack, but they did not express to the War Council and were not asked to express any opinion on the subject, and offered no objection to the naval operations as they considered them experimental and such as could be discontinued if the first results obtained were not satisfactory. Moreover, such objections as they entertained were mainly based on their preference for the adoption of other plans in other theatres of war.

(g) We think that there was an obligation first on the First Lord, secondly on the Prime Minister and thirdly on the other Members of the War Council to see that the views of the Naval Advisers were clearly put before the Council;

we also think that the Naval Advisers should
have expressed their views to the Council,
whether asked or not, if they considered that the
project which the Council was about to adopt
was impracticable from a naval point of view.

(h) Looking at the position which existed on
January 13th, we do not think the War Council
were justified in coming to a decision without
much fuller investigation of the proposition
which had been suggested to them that "the
Admiralty should prepare for a naval expedition
in February to bombard and take the Gallipoli
Peninsula with Constantinople as its objective."
We do not consider that the urgency was such
as to preclude a short adjournment to enable
the Naval and Military advisers of the
Government to make a thorough examination
of the question. We hold that the possibility of
making a surprise amphibious attack on the
Gallipoli Peninsula offered such great military
and political advantages that it was mistaken and
ill-advised to sacrifice this possibility by hastily
deciding to undertake a purely naval attack
which from its nature could not attain
completely the objects set out in the terms of
the decision.

(i) We are led to the conclusion that the decision
taken on February 16th to mass troops in the
neighbourhood of the Dardanelles marked a
very critical stage of the whole operation. It
ought to have been clear at the time that, when

this was once done, although the troops might not have been actually landed, it would become apparent to all the world that a really serious attack was intended, and that withdrawal could no longer be effected without running a serious risk of loss of prestige. We consider that at that moment, inasmuch as time was all-important, no compromise was possible between making an immediate and vigorous effort to ensure success at the Dardanelles by a joint naval and military occupation, or falling back on the original intention of desisting from the naval attack if the experiences gained during the bombardment were not satisfactory.

(j) On the 20th February Lord Kitchener decided that the XXIXth Division, part of the troops which by the decision of February 16th were to have been sent to the East, should not be sent at that time, and Colonel Fitzgerald by his order instructed the Director of Naval Transports that the transports for that division and the rest of the Expeditionary Force would not be required. This was done without informing the First Lord, and the despatch of the troops was thus delayed for three weeks. This delay gravely compromised the probability of success of the original attack made by the land forces, and materially increased the difficulties encountered in the final attack some months later.

(k) We consider that, in view of the opinions expressed by the naval and military authorities on the spot, the decision to abandon the naval attack after the bombardment of March 18th was inevitable.

(l) There was no meeting of the War Council between March 19th and May 14th. Meanwhile important land operations were undertaken. We think that before such operations were commenced the War Council should have carefully reconsidered the whole position. In our opinion the Prime Minister ought to have summoned a meeting of the War Council for that purpose, and if not summoned, the other Members of the War Council should have pressed for such a meeting. We think this was a serious omission.

(m) We consider that the responsibility of those members of the Cabinet who did not attend the meetings of the War Council was limited to the fact that they delegated their authority to their colleagues who attended those meetings.

(n) We are of opinion that Lord Kitchener did not sufficiently avail himself of the services of his General Staff, with the result that more work was undertaken by him than was possible for one man to do, and confusion and want of efficiency resulted.

(o) We are unable to concur in the view set forth by Lord Fisher that it was his duty, if he differed from the Chief of his Department, to maintain silence at the Council or to resign. We think that the adoption of any such principle generally would impair the efficiency of the public service.

(p) We think that, although the main object was not attained, certain important political advantages, upon the nature of which we have already dwelt, were secured by the Dardanelles expedition. Whether those advantages were worth the loss of life and treasure involved is, and must always remain, a matter of opinion.

We cannot close this report without expressing our high appreciation of the services rendered to us both by Sir Maurice Hankey, whose Memoranda, which we have frequently quoted, have been of the utmost service to us, and by our able Secretary, Mr. Grimwood Mears.

All which we humbly report for your Majesty's gracious consideration.

CROMER.

ANDREW FISHER.

THOMAS MACKENZIE.

FREDK. CAWLEY.

J. A. CLYDE.

STEPHEN L. GWYNN.

W. H. MAY.

NICHOLSON.

W. PICKFORD.

E. GRIMWOOD MEARS,
Secretary.
February 12th, 1917.

∞◌◆◌∞

MINUTE OF THE RIGHT HONOURABLE
ANDREW FISHER

I am not in agreement with the majority as regards
the form their Report takes, though I readily recognise they have drawn it up as it is with the sole aim
of helping others who may read it to arrive at the
conclusions they believe to be justified by what they
have seen and heard as Commissioners.

Though I have no rooted objections to the
recitation of introductory events and of established
facts which are necessary for an intelligent

understanding of the points at issue before the Commission, I am of opinion it is unwise for Commissioners (in this case a jury of the nation) to traverse particular portions of the evidence which have led them to arrive at their verdict. I am in a greater difficulty to understand the point of view which, whilst arriving at certain conclusions upon the evidence, cheerfully admits that the perusal of the same evidence may lead other people—not members of the Commission—to other conclusions; the net result suggesting an absence of decision which will go far to destroy the whole value of the findings.

The particular conclusions of the Majority Report from which I dissent are as follows:—

Paragraph "(g) . . . we also think that the Naval Advisers should have expressed their views to the Council, whether asked or not, if they considered that the project which the Council was about to adopt was impracticable from a naval point of view."

Paragraph "(o) We are unable to concur in the view set forth by Lord Fisher that it was his duty, if he differed from the Chief of his Department, to maintain silence at the Council or to resign. We think that the adoption of any such principle generally would impair the efficiency of the public service."

I dissent in the strongest terms from any suggestion that the Departmental Advisers of a Minister in his company at a Council Meeting should express any views at all other than to the Minister and through him, unless specifically invited to do so. I am of opinion it would seal the fate of responsible government if servants of the State were to share the responsibility of Ministers to Parliament and to the people on matters of public policy.

The Minister has command of the opinions and views of all officers of the Department he administers on matters of public policy. Good stewardship demands from Ministers of the Crown frank, fair, full statements of all opinions of trusted experienced officials to colleagues, when they have direct reference to matters of high policy.

ANDREW FISHER.

DISSENT AND SUGGESTION BY THE HONOURABLE SIR THOMAS MACKENZIE, K.C.M.G.

Whilst agreeing that if conclusions are introduced at this stage it is necessary to support them by the descriptive narrative (although, in my opinion, such narrative should not embody the findings arrived at), I take exception to certain conclusions, which should, I think, be struck out of the Report.

We are only at the "Origin and Inception" stage of the inquiry, and it seems to me premature to express any opinion on general results at this point of the proceedings. Sufficient evidence has not been taken to enable us to arrive at a decision on the objects attained by the operations. Connecting this section with paragraph (*p*) of the "Conclusions", I do not think the Commission is as yet justified in reaching the conclusions mentioned. It will be necessary for us to investigate such questions as the conduct of the offensive on the Peninsula, and the carrying out of the various subsidiary operations, etc., before we can estimate with any degree of accuracy the costs involved and form an opinion as to the results of the enterprise, for only then will events assume their true perspective.

Indeed, it may well be that our further investigations will shed a different light on the results attained, and reveal facts which may have the effect of materially altering the judgment expressed in the two paragraphs under notice. They may even demand inquiries being instituted outside the scope of those entrusted to the Commission; and, in any case, it is only after we have brought under review all the available evidence on the Dardanelles campaign as a whole that we shall be able to estimate cost and assess results and also apportion blame or credit where called for or merited.

I also dissent from paragraphs (*g*) and (*o*) of the "Conclusions". I hold that if the Departmental Adviser of a Minister states his opinion to his Minister, he has discharged what may be reasonably considered to be his official duty. And in such a case as we have under notice, where the Minister and his adviser were both present at a meeting of the War Council, I feel that the adviser had fulfilled all that was required of him, seeing that he was not asked to express his views to the meeting. The Minister, and not the adviser, must be regarded as responsible for representing the Departmental view, but in such circumstances the Minister should have stated his adviser's opinion fully to the assembly.

The report shows that this view does not commend itself to the majority of the Commission, and as it is of importance that the opinions of such expert advisers should at all times be readily available and given in connection with the deliberations of the War Committee, and to assist members in arriving at right conclusions, I am of opinion that the Chief of Staff and the First Sea Lord should be appointed members of the War Committee.

THOMAS MACKENZIE.

MINUTE BY MR. ROCH

While I concur in some of the conclusions contained in this report, I regret that I am unable to sign
it.

The conclusions which I have come to, and the
review of the evidence which, I think, justifies
those conclusions are contained in a separate
memorandum.

WALTER ROCH.

22nd *December*, 1916.

MEMORANDUM BY MR. ROCH

Consideration of the scope of the inquiry showed that the story of these operations fell naturally into three chapters. First, the circumstances leading up to the campaign, second, the conception, execution and failure of the plan for forcing the Dardanelles by ships alone, and third, the attempt and failure to take the Gallipoli Peninsula by military operations aided by the Fleet.

This memorandum is presented dealing with the first two Chapters.

The policy and higher direction of the war, during the period under review, were in the hands of a body known as the War Council. This body—a development of the Committee of Imperial Defence—consisted of the following Cabinet Ministers:—

> Mr. Asquith (Prime Minister).
> Lord Haldane (Lord Chancellor).
> Lord Kitchener (Secretary of State for War).
> Mr. Lloyd George (Chancellor of the Exchequer).
> Sir E. Grey (Secretary of State for Foreign Affairs).
> Mr. Churchill (First Lord of the Admiralty), and
> Lord Crewe (Secretary of State for India).

Its Councils were attended regularly by Mr. A. J. Balfour, Lord Fisher, Sir Arthur Wilson, Sir Jas. Wolfe Murray and Lt.-Col. Hankey, who acted as Secretary.

Particular meetings were attended by other Cabinet Ministers and various officers, including Sir John French, the Commander-in-Chief of the British Forces in France.

During the same period the naval strategy of the war was controlled by a body known as "The War Group" presided over by Mr. Churchill as First Lord and consisting of:—

> Lord Fisher (First Sea Lord).
> Admiral Oliver (Chief of the Staff).

Admiral of the Fleet, Sir A. Wilson, and
Commander de Bartolomé (Naval Secretary to
Mr. Churchill).

The consultations of this body were on occasions attended by Sir Henry Jackson, who was serving on Admiral Oliver's staff.

The Board of Admiralty occupied a subordinate position. Its members (other than Mr. Churchill and Lord Fisher) were not consulted on naval policy or even kept well-informed on naval events. They were merely managers of the different departments assigned to them.

At the War Councils Mr. Churchill was the spokesman of the Admiralty, attended by Lord Fisher and Sir Arthur Wilson.

Lord Fisher and Sir Arthur Wilson both insisted that they were not members of this Council in the same sense as the Cabinet Ministers who were present. They considered themselves to be merely naval advisers, and only entitled to express their opinions when asked for them.

Neither Mr. Churchill nor the Cabinet Ministers who were members of the Council accepted this view, and were equally insistent that they assumed the assent of both Lord Fisher and Sir Arthur Wilson to be implied unless they expressed their dissent.

The military strategy and conduct of the war were under the complete and sole control of Lord Kitchener. He, in effect, combined in himself the functions and duties of Secretary of State and

Commander-in-Chief. Under his régime the General Staff was not consulted and really ceased to exist.

Lord Kitchener was attended at the War Council by Sir James Wolfe Murray, the Chief of the Imperial General Staff.

At these Councils Sir Jas. Wolfe Murray stated that he neither gave nor was asked for any opinion.

The problem of forcing the Dardanelles had been considered in recent years on different occasions and under varying circumstances:—

(*a*) By Lord Fisher when the Mediterranean Fleet under his command lay at Lemnos during the South African War.

(*b*) By Lord Fisher in 1904 when as First Sea Lord he satisfied himself that "even with military co-operation the operation was mightily hazardous."

(*c*) By the Committee of Imperial Defence in 1906. The General Staff was then opposed to any naval or military action at the Dardanelles.

This view was substantially concurred in by the Director of Naval Intelligence, the sole difference of opinion recorded between the General Staff and the Director of Naval Intelligence being that:—

"While the former appear to regard the enterprise in question as too hazardous, the latter, while recognising the great risk involved, is of opinion that it is within the bounds of possibility that an operation of this nature might be forced upon us ... and that in such an event there is no reason to despair of success, though at the expense, in all likelihood, of heavy sacrifices."

The possibility of an attack on the Dardanelles was discussed, for the first time, at a War Council on 25th November, 1914.*

Mr. Churchill then expressed the view that the best way of defending Egypt was an attack on some part of the coast of Asiatic Turkey, and suggested an attack on the Gallipoli Peninsula, which, if successful, would give us the control of the Dardanelles, and enable us to dictate terms at Constantinople.

A feint attack on the Gallipoli Peninsula—the real objective being some other point on the Turkish Coast—was discussed.

Owing to the shortage of merchant shipping, occasioned largely by military demands, the project was put on one side.

By the end of November, 1914, the great German effort to reach the Channel Ports had been defeated at the first battle of Ypres, and a winter lull set in during the succeeding weeks.

The end of 1914, and the beginning of 1915, was spent by the War Council in attempts to arrive at their

---

* Turkey had declared war against Britain on 31st October 1914.

future military policy, and to make plans for the employment of the new armies in the Spring.

On the 28th December, 1914, a memorandum was circulated to the members of the War Council by Sir Maurice Hankey.

This memorandum called attention to the "remarkable deadlock" which had occurred in the Western theatre of war. It invited consideration of the possibility of seeking some other outlet for the effective employment of the new armies. It further suggested that Germany could perhaps "be struck most effectively, and with the most lasting results on the peace of the world, through her Allies, and particularly Turkey." And asked the question whether it was not possible "now to weave a web around Turkey, which will end her career as a European power?"

This was followed on the 1st January by a memorandum from Mr. Lloyd George also pointing to the East as the true objective and outlining a far-reaching policy directed against Austria in co-operation with the Greeks, Roumanians and Serbians, and also against Turkey.

Other plans and policies were discussed, producing three schools of thought at the War Council.

(*a*) One school holding that all efforts should be concentrated in the Western theatre of war, since there and there alone could decisive success be achieved.

(*b*) A second school maintaining that a complete deadlock had already set in the West and advising operations designed to obtain the support of Italy and Roumania against Austria, secure Greek co-operation, and achieve the destruction of Turkey as a European power.

(*c*) A third school advocating the intermediate view that the theory of a complete deadlock in the West was not yet proved or disproved, and that our main military efforts should be concentrated on the Western line until failure showed the necessity of seeking other theatres.

It is remarkable that none of these various policies and plans were ever discussed by the War Council in the light of written detailed staff estimates of men and munitions.

While the minds of the members of the War Council were engaged on these general discussions, on the 2nd January, 1915, a telegram was received at the Foreign Office from the British Ambassador at Petrograd conveying a request from the [Russian Military Authorities] to Lord Kitchener, that a Naval or Military demonstration against the Turks should be arranged in order to relieve the pressure felt by the Russian Troops at the Caucasus.

To this telegram, Lord Kitchener on his own initiative replied through the Foreign Office on the following day, promising to make a demonstration, but expressing a doubt as to whether any such steps would cause any serious withdrawal by Turkish troops.

On the 2nd January, the position was discussed by

Lord Kitchener and Mr. Churchill and Lord Kitchener then asked Mr. Churchill if the Navy could make a demonstration at the Dardanelles.

Lord Kitchener on the same day in a letter to Mr. Churchill expressed the view that he did not see "that we can do anything that will seriously help the Russians in the Caucasus ... We have no troops to land anywhere. The only place that a demonstration might have any effect in stopping reinforcements going East would be the Dardanelles ... We shall not be ready for anything big for some months."

Simultaneously Lord Fisher expressed his view of the position in a private letter to Mr. Churchill. "I consider the attack on Turkey holds the field, but only if it is immediate; however, it won't be. We shall decide on a futile bombardment of the Dardanelles, which wears out the invaluable guns of the 'Indefatigable', which probably will require replacement. What good resulted from the last bombardment? Did it move a single Turk from the Caucasus?"

And he concluded by sketching out an ambitious policy requiring the co-operation of Roumania, Bulgaria, Greece and Serbia, and necessitating the withdrawal of substantial forces from France.

On the 4th January, Lord Fisher further embodied his views in a formal Minute to Mr. Churchill.

"It seems necessary to lay down in the first place what the British Naval policy is:

(*a*) In the first place that policy is to conserve
our naval superiority over the Germans, and
in no wise jeopardise by minor operations,
whose cumulative effect is to wear out our
vessels, and incur losses in ships and men.
We cannot afford any more losses or any
further deterioration, except for absolutely
imperative operations.

(*b*) The naval advantages of the possession of
Constantinople, and the getting of wheat
from the Black Sea, are so overwhelming
that I consider Colonel Hankey's plans for
Turkish operations vital and imperative, and
very pressing."

During the next few days, the following
telegrams were exchanged between Mr. Churchill
and Admiral Carden, who was then in command of
the Mediterranean Fleet.

(1) 3rd January: From Mr. Churchill to Admiral
Carden:—

"Are you of opinion that it is practicable to
force the Dardanelles by the use of ships alone?
It is assumed that older battleships would be
employed, that they would be furnished with
mine sweepers, and that they would be preceded
by colliers or other merchant vessels as sweepers,
and the importance of the results would justify
severe losses. Let me know what your views
are."

(2) January 5th: From Admiral Carden to Mr.
  Churchill:—

  "I do not think that the Dardanelles can be
  rushed, but they might be forced by extended
  operations with a large number of ships."

(3) January 6th: From Mr. Churchill to Admiral
  Carden:—

  "High authorities here concur in your opinion.
  Forward detailed particulars showing what force
  would be required for extended operations.
  How do you think it should be employed, and
  what results can be gained?"

Admiral Oliver, though doubtful, if he saw this last
telegram, did concur with it.

Lord Fisher did not see it.

Sir Henry Jackson did not remember whether he
was consulted with regard to it or not.

Mr. Churchill explained that by "high authorities" he did not include Lord Fisher, and that he
meant Sir Henry Jackson and Admiral Oliver.

Admiral Carden understood Mr. Churchill to
include either Lord Fisher or Sir Henry Jackson or
both.

By the 5th of January Sir Henry Jackson had
completed a Memorandum in accordance with instructions given to him by Mr. Churchill on the 3rd.

It was not seen by Mr. Churchill until some days
later.

This Memorandum was in the main directed to
the possibility of rushing the Dardanelles, and entered

into minute details of the force required, and the losses which would be involved in "reaching the Straits."

It contained also the following observations under the heading of "General Remarks."

"Assuming the enemy squadron destroyed and the batteries rushed, they would be open to the fire of field artillery and infantry, and to torpedo attack at night, with no store ships with ammunition, and no retreat without re-engaging the shore batteries, unless those had been destroyed when forcing the passage.

Though they might dominate the city and inflict enormous damage, their position would not be an enviable one unless there was a large military force to occupy the town.

Strategically such a diversion would only be carried out when the object to be gained was commensurate with the loss the fleet would sustain in forcing the passage.

The actual capture of Constantinople would be worth a considerable loss, but the bombardment alone would not greatly affect the distant military operations, and even if it surrendered, it could not be occupied and held without troops, and would probably result in indiscriminate massacres."

This memorandum was not circulated to the members of the War Council.

Sir Henry Jackson insisted in his evidence that he

had "always stuck" to this memorandum: "that it would be a very mad thing to try and get into the Sea of Marmora without having the Gallipoli Peninsula held by our own troops or every gun on both sides of the Straits destroyed. He had never changed that opinion and he had never given any one any reason to think he had."

Admiral Carden's reply to Mr. Churchill's telegram of 6th January was received on the 11th January. This telegram suggested four successive operations as being possible:

(*a*) The destruction of defences at the entrance to the Dardanelles.

(*b*) Action inside the Straits, so as to clear the defences up to and including Cephez Point, Battery No. 8.

(*c*) The destruction of defences of the Narrows.

(*d*) Sweeping of a clear channel through the minefield, and advance through the Narrows followed by a reduction of forts farther up, and advance into the Sea of Marmora.

And estimated that a month would be necessary to carry out these operations.

This telegram was immediately circulated to the members of the War Council.

Admiral Carden stated in his evidence that he "had it in his mind that it was impossible to form a real opinion on the subject until one had destroyed the outer forts at the entrance and was able to get inside and actually find out the extent of the gun defences, of the minefield, and the extent of the movable armament on both sides of the Straits." But there is no indication of this view in any of his telegrams to the Admiralty.

Admiral Carden's plan was then discussed by the members of the War Group at the Admiralty at their daily consultations.

Their views were not expressed in any written memoranda, and it is, therefore, difficult to state precisely what those views were.

I think there was no real consensus of favourable opinion.

Lord Fisher told us that he "was instinctively against it," and that to a large extent "having expressed his indisposition to have much to do with it, he more or less left it alone. Sir Henry Jackson was a very able man and so was Admiral Oliver, and he (Lord Fisher) more or less stood aside. He backed it up in every possible way so far as executive work was concerned."

Sir Arthur Wilson stated that "he never recommended it. He never strongly resisted it because it was not his business to do so, but so far as he did remark on it he was against it," and that "the question of the Dardanelles had never been put to him definitely at all. Sir Henry Jackson was working at the details of the scheme and he (Sir A. Wilson) was looking at the details of others."

Admiral Oliver stated that "his opinion always was that we might go a certain length by naval attack but it would depend on the resistance that the enemy made and the state of their defences how far we could go," and that he would have preferred not "stirring the place up until it had been decided to make a proper attempt, that is to say to make a big attempt with Army and Navy."

Commodore Bartolomé stated that "his view had always been that it should be a combined operation, but he thought that if the Dardanelles were attacked by a purely naval force a certain proportion, probably not more than half, could get through ... but having got through he did not see what they could do."

All were agreed in thinking that the proposed operations could not lead to disaster as they could be broken off at any moment. All assumed that the War Council looked upon immediate action as a political necessity, and that no troops for a joint operation could be obtained.

Sir Henry Jackson was not a member of the War Group, though he was present at some of the meetings at which the proposed operations were discussed. He alone expressed his views in writing.

Those views are contained in the memorandum of the 5th January, which has been referred to, and in a further memorandum of the 15th January, in which he deals specifically with Admiral Carden's plan.

On the 12th January Lord Fisher suggested the possible employment of the "Queen Elizabeth" in the proposed operations, in the following minute to Admiral Oliver:—

"I have told Crease to find out from Percy Scott and the gunnery experts of anything to prevent 'Queen Elizabeth' firing all her ammunition at the Dardanelles forts instead of uselessly into the sea at Gibraltar and to let you know. If this is practicable she could go straight there, hoist Carden's flag, and go on with her exercises and free the 'Indefatigable' to Malta for refit and allow 'Inflexible' to go straight from Gibraltar to join the second Battle Cruiser Squadron."

On the same day Admiral Oliver also received a minute from Mr. Churchill, which was formally concurred in by Lord Fisher, and was in the following terms:—

"The forcing of the Dardanelles as proposed and the arrival of a squadron strong enough to defeat the Turkish fleet in the Sea of Marmora would be a victory of first importance and change to our advantage the whole situation of the war in the East. It would appear possible to provide the force required by Admiral Carden without weakening the margin necessary in home waters."

The minute then gave full details of the ships to be employed and concluded by saying:—

"All arrangements should be secretly concerted for carrying the plan through, the sea-planes and auxiliary craft being provided, Admiral Carden to command ... definite plans should be worked out accordingly."

On the 13th January, 1915, Admiral Carden's plan was unfolded in detail by Mr. Churchill to the War Council.

He concluded, in the words of Sir M. Hankey's Note, by stating that "the Admiralty were studying the question and believed that a plan could be made for systematically reducing all the forts within a few weeks. Once the forts were reduced the minefields would be cleared, and the Fleet would proceed up to Constantinople and destroy the 'Goeben.' They would have nothing to fear from field guns or rifles, which would be merely an inconvenience."

At this Council, Lord Fisher and Sir Arthur Wilson expressed no opinion.

The actual decision come to was that:

"The Admiralty should prepare for a naval expedition in February to bombard and take the Gallipoli Peninsula, with Constantinople as its objective."

At this Council it was assumed that no troops were available, and this was accentuated by the fact that the Council on the same day sanctioned a plan of Sir John French's for offensive military operations in France.

This decision by the War Council set the mechanism of the Admiralty in motion.

The plan of attack was communicated to the French, the co-operation of a French squadron was sought, and arrangements were made for the command by a British Admiral.

A Fleet concentration scheme was prepared by the Chief of the Admiralty War Staff.

All these preparations were made through the ordinary routine of the Admiralty. They were concurred in by Lord Fisher, who himself added the "Lord Nelson" and "Agamemnon" to the Fleet allocated to the operations.

On the 14th January the abandonment of a subsidiary naval bombardment in the East was recommended by Mr. Churchill in a formal minute to the Prime Minister.

This Minute, which was concurred in by Lord Fisher, was in the following terms:

"The attack on the Dardanelles will require practically our whole available margin. If that attack opens prosperously, it will very soon attract to itself the whole attention of the Eastern theatre, and if it succeeds, it will produce results which will undoubtedly influence every Mediterranean power.
"In these circumstances we strongly advise ... that we should devote ourselves to ... the methodical forcing of the Dardanelles."

On the 15th January, Sir Henry Jackson completed a memorandum on Admiral Carden's plan.

This memo began with the words—"Concur generally in his (*i.e.* Admiral Carden's) plans. Our previous appreciations of the situation differed only in small details."

It then dealt in detail with the two first operations (*a*) and (*b*) outlined by Admiral Carden's plan. Suggesting that when these had been attempted "the experience thus gained would show the practicability of continuing this direct attack on other forts in the Narrows," and ended by suggesting that "(*a*) might be approved at once as the experience gained would be useful."

Sir Henry Jackson insisted that in this memorandum he recommended only an attack on the outer forts.

He also insisted that when he prepared his memorandum he accepted the policy of a purely naval attack. To use his own words: "It was not for me to decide. I had no responsibilities whatever as to the decision. I had no responsibilities except just for the staff work which I did." And he stated further that he gave his expert advice on Admiral Carden's plan "if it was approved to do it. Whether the game was worth the candle is another thing."

This memorandum, though it was read by Mr. Churchill at the War Council of the 28th January, was not circulated to the members.

The plans for the purely Naval attack were thus maturing.

As the time for final decision by the War Council drew near, Lord Fisher's attitude of passive dislike developed into one of active hostility.

On the 25th January, he took the very unusual

step of submitting a Memorandum on Naval Policy direct to the Prime Minister.

This Memorandum, Mr. Churchill stated, gave him the first indication "that the First Sea Lord had, since the first meeting of the War Council, developed serious misgivings about it."

Lord Fisher's memorandum was in two parts.

The second part contained the outline of a large naval scheme which was directed to what seemed to Lord Fisher a more decisive theatre of the war, and which had been his main pre-occupation.

The first part set forth Lord Fisher's objections to the proposed operations in the Dardanelles as being opposed to what he conceived to be the British Naval Policy.

The following extracts sufficiently illustrate those views:

"They (*i.e.* the Germans) have already endeavoured without success to scatter our naval strength by attacks on our trade and not much more successfully to reduce our main strength by submarines and mines."

"Pressure of sea power ... is still a slow process and requires great patience. In time it will almost certainly compel the enemy to seek a decision at sea, particularly when he begins to realise that his offensive on land is broken. This is one reason for husbanding our resources.

Another reason is that the prolongation of

war at sea tends to raise up fresh enemies for the dominant naval power in a much higher degree than it does on land owing to the exasperation of neutrals. The tendency will only be checked by the conviction of an overwhelming naval supremacy behind the nation exercising sea power.

The sole justification of coastal bombardments and attacks by the fleet on fortified places, such as the contemplated prolonged bombardment of the Dardanelles forts by our fleet, is to force a decision at sea, and so far and no further can they be justified.

So long as the German High Sea Fleet possesses its present great strength and splendid gunnery efficiency, so long is it imperative, and indeed vital, that no operation whatever should be undertaken by the British Fleet calculated to impair its present superiority, which is none too great in view of the heavy losses already experienced in valuable ships and invaluable officers and men whose places cannot be filled in the period of the war (in which respect the Navy differs so materially from the Army).

Even the older ships should not be risked, for they cannot be lost without losing men, and they form the only reserve behind the Grand Fleet."

Mr. Churchill at once himself drafted a reply to Lord

Fisher which was also submitted to the Prime
Minister.

This memorandum contained an elaborate analy-
sis of the comparative strength of the British and
German Navies, showing that for all existing purposes
the margin of the British fleet for all requirements
was, in Mr. Churchill's opinion, ample and even overwhelming.

It concluded with the following general reply to
Lord Fisher's argument.

"It is believed that, with care and skill, losses
may be reduced to a minimum, and certainly
kept within limits fully justified by the
importance and necessity of the operations. It
cannot be said that this employment of ships
which are (except the 'Duncans') not needed
and not suited to fight in the line of battle,
conflicts with any of the sound principles of
naval policy set forth by the First Sea Lord. Not
to use them where necessary because of some
fear that there will be an outcry if a ship is lost
would be wrong, and, if a certain proportion of
loss of life among officers and men of the
Royal Navy on these ships can achieve
important objects of the war and save a very
much greater loss of life among our comrades
and allies on shore, we ought certainly not to
shrink from it."

Lord Fisher had also intimated to Mr. Churchill that

he was not going to the War Council, as he did not like "this Dardanelles affair."

On the night of the 27th January, Lord Fisher was informed that the Prime Minister considered it imperative that Lord Fisher should be in his private room with Mr. Churchill half an hour before the War Council began. They met as arranged on the morning of the 28th. It is impossible to expect, after so long a lapse of time, an actual reproduction of what took place at this interview.

My view of the evidence is that Lord Fisher left the room under the impression that the Prime Minister was in favour of the proposed operations at the Dardanelles and that the Prime Minister had formed the conclusion that Lord Fisher's objections were due to his preference for his own alternative scheme as a matter of high policy, and were not directed against the practicability of the operations.

The Prime Minister, Mr. Churchill and Lord Fisher then went at once to the meeting of the War Council.

The following is the note of what occurred supplied to us by Sir Maurice Hankey:—

"Mr. Churchill informed the War Council that he had communicated to the Grand Duke Nicholas and to the French Admiralty the project for a naval attack on the Dardanelles. The Grand Duke had replied with enthusiasm, and believed that this might assist him. The

French Admiralty had also sent a favourable reply, and had promised co-operation. Preparations were in hand for commencing about the middle of February.

Mr. Churchill asked if the War Council attached importance to this operation, which undoubtedly involved some risks.

There was no hostile criticism, though Lord Fisher said that he had understood that this question would not be raised to-day, and that the Prime Minister was well aware of his own views with regard to it.

To this the Prime Minister replied in the sense that, in view of the steps which had been taken, the question could not well be left in abeyance.

Apart from this the opinions expressed were entirely favourable to the enterprise.

Among the advantages claimed for it were that—

It would cut the Turkish Army in two.
It would put Constantinople under our control.
It would finally settle the attitude of Bulgaria and the whole of the Balkans.
It would give us the advantage of having the Russian wheat, and enable Russia to resume exports. (This would restore the Russian exchanges which were falling, owing to her inability to export, and causing great embarrassment.)

It would open a passage to the Danube.
If successful, its effect would be equivalent
to that of a successful compaign fought with
the new armies.

One merit of the scheme was that, if
satisfactory progress was not made, the
attack could be broken off.

The War Council were informed by Mr.
Churchill that the naval Commander-in-Chief in
the Mediterranean had expressed his belief that it
could be done. He required from three weeks to
a month to accomplish it. The necessary ships
were already on their way to the Dardanelles. He
also said that, in response to his inquiries, the
French had expressed their confidence that
Austrian Submarines would not get as far as the
Dardanelles, and that, so far as could be
ascertained, the Turks had no submarines. He did
not anticipate that we should sustain much loss
in the actual bombardment, but in sweeping the
mines some losses must be expected. The real
difficulties would begin after the outer forts had
been silenced, and it became necessary to attack
the Narrows.

Mr. Churchill fully explained the plan of
attack on a map."

To this account one incident—not without dra-
matic intensity—must be added. Lord Fisher learnt in
the course of the discussion that a final decision was
being come to.

"Thereupon (to quote from a note made by Lord Fisher at the time) Lord Fisher left the Council table, followed by Lord Kitchener, who asked Lord Fisher what he intended to do. Lord Fisher replied to Lord Kitchener that he would not return to the Council table and would resign his office as First Sea Lord. Lord Kitchener then urged on Lord Fisher that he (Lord Fisher) was the only dissentient, that the Dardanelles operations had been decided upon by the Prime Minister, and he put it to Lord Fisher that his duty to his Country was to carry on the duties of First Sea Lord. Lord Fisher, after further conversation, reluctantly gave in to Lord Kitchener's entreaty and resumed his seat."

This incident had not escaped the attention of Mr. Churchill, who felt, to use his own words, that he "must come to a clear understanding with the First Sea Lord." They met after the adjournment of the War Council in Mr. Churchill's room. Mr. Churchill strongly urged Lord Fisher to undertake the operations.

Lord Fisher definitely consented.

Accompanied by Admiral Oliver, in place of Sir A. Wilson, they then repaired to the afternoon meeting of the War Council. At the close of this meeting Mr. Churchill stated that the Admiralty had decided to push on with the project to make a naval attack on the Dardanelles.

It is remarkable to have to record:

(*a*) That Lord Fisher's memorandum and Mr. Churchill's reply were not placed before the War Council at these meetings.

(*b*) That no members of the Council—other than the Prime Minister, Mr. Churchill and Lord Fisher—knew until a later date of the discussion which had preceded their deliberations.

Lord Fisher insisted in his evidence that he had taken every step—short of resignation—to show his dislike of the proposed operations.

He told us "that in his judgment it is not the business of the chief technical advisers of the Government to resign because their advice is not accepted unless they are of opinion that the operations proposed must lead to disastrous results. The attempt to force the Dardanelles as a purely naval operation would not have been disastrous so long as the ships employed could be withdrawn at any moment, and only such vessels were engaged, as in the beginning of the operations was in fact the case, as could be spared without detriment to the general service of the fleet."

In answer to the question why he made no protest at the meetings of the War Council, Lord Fisher further stated:—

"Mr. Churchill knew my opinion. I did not think it would tend towards good relations between the First Lord and myself nor to the smooth working of the Board of Admiralty to raise objections in the War Council's discussions. My opinion being known to Mr. Churchill in what I regarded as the proper constitutional way, I preferred thereafter to remain silent."

When on the 14th May the War Council decided to continue the operations at the Dardanelles and to divert further ships for the purpose Lord Fisher thought that his great alternative scheme, which had been his main pre-occupation during this period, and to which his mind and energies had been almost exclusively devoted, was doomed. To use his own words again: "It seemed to me that I was faced at last by a progressive frustration of my main schemes of naval strategy."

On the following day he resigned his post as First Sea Lord.

The decision of the War Council was then translated into action.

The Plan of operations was finally approved by M. Augagneur (the French Minister of Marine), who pronounced them to be "prudent et prévoyant."

The final arrangements for the naval attack were completed and a detailed staff paper on the proposed operations were sent by the Admiralty to Admiral Carden on the 5th February.

On the 17th or 18th of February the Prime Minister conveyed to the Cabinet the unanimous decision of the War Council. It was accepted by them without question, criticism, or discussion of any kind. The bombardment opened on the 19th February.

Attention has been called to the varying schools

of thought which existed in the War Council at the beginning of 1915.

During the ensuing weeks what may be called the Eastern school of thought gained strength under the shadow of the threatened Austro-German attack on Serbia, the coming offensive against Russia, the failure of our diplomacy in the Balkans due to the want of military success, and the growing appreciation of the fact that the naval attack on the Dardanelles might after all be fruitless without considerable military support.

In the course of the discussions which then took place rival plans and policies were constantly before the Council.

But I am unable to find that the War Council ever really faced or ever really decided whether it was within their power to undertake military operations on a large scale in another theatre of war, or that the great and obvious political advantages to be gained by operations in the East were ever considered in the light of military possibility.

This was due to the complete absence during their discussions of detailed staff estimates in terms of munitions and men, and to the too confident belief in the success of the purely naval attack on the Dardanelles, in the chance of an ineffective Turkish resistance and in the decisive effect of the appearance of the Fleet off Constantinople.

Early in February a proposal was made that a British and French division should be sent to Salonica to support Serbia in conjunction with the Greeks.

Lord Kitchener was ready to send the XXIXth division and expressed the opinion that it would be very useful to the Navy in their attack on the Dardanelles to have some good troops at Salonica.

On the 15th February this scheme ultimately broke down owing to the lack of Greek co-operation.

Meanwhile the necessity for troops to support the Naval attack grew more apparent.

It was emphasized by a memorandum which Sir Henry Jackson had completed on the 15th February and sent, by way of suggestion, to Admiral Carden.

This memo, while giving detailed notes on the proposed operations, concluded with the following general remarks:—

"The provision of the necessary military forces to enable the fruits of this heavy naval undertaking to be gathered must never be lost sight of; the transports carrying them should be in readiness to enter the Straits as soon as it is seen the forts at the Narrows will be silenced.

To complete this destruction strong military landing parties with strong covering forces will be necessary.

It is considered, however, that the full advantage of the undertaking would only be obtained by the occupation of the Peninsula by a military force acting in conjunction with the naval operations, as the pressure of a strong field army of the enemy on the Peninsula would not only greatly harass the operations, but would render the passage of the Straits impracticable by any but powerfully-armed vessels, even though all the permanent defences had been silenced."

The naval bombardment is not recommended as a sound military operation unless a strong military force is ready to assist in the operation, or at least, follow it up immediately the forts are silenced."

On the 16th February the War Council came to the following decision:—

"(1) The XXIXth Division, hitherto intended to form part of Sir John French's Army, to be dispatched to Lemnos at the earliest possible date. It is hoped that it may be able to sail within nine or ten days.

(2) Arrangements to be made for a force to be dispatched from Egypt, if required.

(3) The whole of the above forces, in conjunction with the battalions of the Royal Marines already dispatched, to be available in case of necessity to support the naval attack on the Dardanelles.

(4) Horse boats to be taken out with the XXIXth division, and the Admiralty to make arrangements to collect small craft, tugs and lighters in the Levant.

(5) The Admiralty to build special transports and

> lighters suitable for the conveyance and
> landing of 50,000 men at any point when
> they may be required."

This decision marks a great development of the plan which had been sanctioned by the War Council of the 28th January.

Confidence still existed that the Fleet would force the Dardanelles and that local military operations would only be necessary to complete the demolition of the forts and deal with concealed howitzers.

But the idea grew steadily that the character of these operations was extending, and that considerable forces (estimated by Lord Kitchener on the 19th February at three divisions) would be necessary to secure the passage of the Dardanelles after the fall of the forts.

Side by side with the development of the original plan, referred to in the last paragraph, there grew up also the idea that it would be impossible for reasons of prestige and policy to break off operations in the event of the failure of the Fleet.

The notes of the War Council show that on the 24th of February, Lord Kitchener felt

> "that if the Fleet would not get through the
> Straits unaided, the Army ought to see the
> business through. The effect of a defeat in the
> Orient would be very serious. There could be
> no going back. The publicity of the
> announcement had committed us."

And that Sir E. Grey expressed the view that "Failure would be equivalent to a great defeat on land."

But that a different opinion was given by Mr. Lloyd George who:

> "strongly urged that the Army should not be required or expected to pull the chestnuts out of the fire for the Navy and that if the Navy failed, we should try somewhere else, in the Balkans, and not necessarily at the Dardanelles."

The necessary steps to concentrate troops in the Mediterranean went forward.

On the 20th of February, the two Australian and New Zealand divisions in Egypt were prepared for service at the Dardanelles, and placed under the command of General Birdwood. Transports were arranged for them and for the XXIXth division and the Naval division at home. By the end of February, a French division was ready to embark.

The naval division sailed on the 3rd of March.

On the 20th of February, Lord Kitchener, on his own initiative, without communicating with Mr. Churchill, cancelled the transports for the XXIXth division. And, owing to his anxiety as to the position in France, would not consent to its release until the 10th of March.

This action by Lord Kitchener led to a strong protest on the part of Mr. Churchill, who at a War Council on the 26th of February asked "that it might be placed on record that he dissented altogether from the retention of the XXIXth division in this country. If a disaster occurred in Turkey owing to the insufficiency of troops, he said he must disclaim all responsibility."

On the 23rd February, General Birdwood was ordered to proceed to the Dardanelles to confer with Admiral Carden.

General Birdwood then made a reconnaissance of the position, and from the telegrams which passed between him and Lord Kitchener it is clear:—

(a) That Lord Kitchener still intended that troops should be used for minor operations only.

(b) That General Birdwood did not expect that the Navy would be able to force the passage of the Straits unaided.

(c) But that General Birdwood fully appreciated the formidable character of the defences of the Peninsula and anticipated that major military operations would be necessary.

These telegrams, however, were not circulated to the members of the War Council.

On the 10th of March, Lord Kitchener announced to the War Council the approximate strength of the forces available against Constantinople [*supplied in table*].

At this Council, Mr. Churchill informed the members that the Admiralty still believed that they could effect the passage of the Straits by naval means alone, but they were glad to know that military support was available if required.

	All ranks	Guns	Horses
Naval Division	11,000	6	1,266
Australian Infantry	30,600	64	9,370
Australian Mounted Troops	3,500	12	4,000
XXIXth Division	18,000	56	5,400
French Division	18,000	40	5,000
Russian Army Corps	47,600	120	10,750
	128,700	298	35,786

On the 12th March, Sir Ian Hamilton was nominated to command these forces, and left for the Dardanelles on the 13th. He was assisted by no staff preparation, and no preliminary scheme of operations of any kind. And it was still assumed that the Navy would force the passage of the Straits.

While the concentration of troops was being made in the Mediterranean, and the events which have been described were taking place in the Councils at home, the naval attack at the Dardanelles was proceeding.

The details of this attack, and the gallantry displayed by the naval forces are well known.

The attack on the outer forts began on the 19th February and was completed on the 25th, though when the demolition parties landed they found 70 per cent. of the heavy guns in a serviceable condition, and had to blow them up with guncotton.

Mine-sweepers were then able to enter and sweep the lower reaches of the Straits. The ships of the fleet entered on the 27th, and attacked Fort Dardanus, which was sufficiently damaged on the 1st and 2nd of March to make sweeping possible up to within 3,000 yards of Cephez Point.

The success of this first attack at once produced important diplomatic results. The eyes of the Balkan nations were fixed on the Dardanelles.

On March 1st the British Minister in Athens telegraphed that M. Venizelos proposed to offer the co-operation of a Greek army corps of three divisions in the Gallipoli Peninsula. He telegraphed again on the 2nd that this proposal had been made after the King had already been "sounded," and that he heard from another source that the King "wanted war."

Within a fortnight Intelligence reports showed that the Turks were moving back to Adrianople and developing their front against Bulgaria.

On March 17th General Paget, who was engaged on a special mission in the Balkans, telegraphed to Lord Kitchener that—

"The operations in the Dardanelles have made a deep impression; that all possibilities of Bulgaria attacking any Balkan State that might side with the *Entente* is now over, and there is some reason to think that shortly the Bulgarian Army will move against Turkey to co-operate in the Dardanelles operations."

Meanwhile the progress of the Fleet in the early days of March was slow.

On the 7th the forts at the Narrows were engaged, but with only partial success, and sweeping made no progress.

Trawlers and destroyers were then sent by night above the mine-fields so that they might sweep down with the current. They came under the enemy's searchlights and were exposed to a terrible fire. The Turkish mobile armament began to develop with harassing effect on the sweepers. The results were small, few mines being exposed or destroyed.

This slow progress was watched by the Admiralty with anxious eyes.

The following telegrams were then exchanged between the Admiralty and Admiral Carden:—

"101. March 11.
Personal and Secret. From First Lord to Vice-Admiral, Eastern Mediterranean.

Caution and deliberate methods were emphasised in your original instructions (and the skill and patience which has enabled your progress to be carried thus far without loss are highly appreciated.)

If, however, success cannot be obtained without loss of ships and men, results to be gained are important enough to justify such a loss. The whole operation may be decided and consequences of a decisive character upon the war may be produced by the turning of the corner Chanak; and we suggest for your consideration, that a point has now been reached when it is necessary to choose favourable weather conditions to overwhelm forts of the Narrows at decisive range by bringing to bear upon them the fire of the largest possible number of guns, great and small. Under cover of this fire landing parties might destroy the guns of the forts, and sweeping operations to clear as much as possible of the minefield might also be carried out.

It might be necessary to repeat the operation until the destruction of all the forts at the Narrows and the clearing of the approaches of mines had been accomplished.

We have no wish to hurry you or urge you beyond your judgment, but we recognise clearly that at a certain period in your operations you will have to press hard for a decision and we desire to know whether, in your opinion, that period has now arrived. Every well-conceived action for forcing a decision, even should regrettable losses be entailed, will receive our support.

Before you take any decisive departure from the present policy we wish to hear your views."

"13 March.
105. From First Lord to Vice-Admiral, Mediterranean.
From the above it is evident that methodical and resolute conduct of the operations by night and day should be pursued, the inevitable losses

being accepted. The enemy is harassed and anxious now. Interference with submarines will be a very serious complication. Time is of the essence."

"13 March.

From Vice-Admiral, Eastern Mediterranean, to Admiralty:—

Your 101 is fully concurred in by me. I consider stage when vigorous sustained action is necessary for success has now been reached. I am of opinion that in order to ensure my communication line immediately fleet enters Sea of Marmora military operations on a large scale should be opened at once."

On the 16th March Admiral Carden was compelled by the advice of the Medical Officer to go on the Sick List.

On the 17th March Admiral de Robeck was appointed in his place. He was asked by the First Lord to give the operations suggested in the telegrams to Admiral Carden his "separate and independent judgment;" to which he expressed his full concurrence.

The great Naval attack began on the 18th.

This attack, although carried out with much skill and gallantry, met with little or no success and resulted in the following damage being done to the Fleet:—

The "Irresistible," the "Ocean" and the "Bouvet"

lost. The "Inflexible" had various compartments flooded, and at one time was in danger of sinking.

The "Suffren" was also hit below water, and had to be docked. The "Gaulois" was badly damaged and had to be beached on Drepana Island.

The "Charlemagne" had her stoke-hold flooded; the "Agamemnon" had one 12-inch gun damaged. The "Lord Nelson" had one 9.2-inch gun put out of action; the "Albion's" foreturret was put out of action for some days.

Thus, out of the 16 attacking ships, three were sunk, and four others so severely damaged that they had to be docked. In spite of these losses Admiral de Robeck telegraphed to the Admiralty on the following day that the squadron "was ready for immediate action except as regards ships lost and damaged but it was necessary to reconsider the plan of attack."

News of these events reached the Admiralty on the following day.

Lord Fisher and Sir A. Wilson, when consulted by Mr. Churchill, were determined to continue the attack.

Lord Fisher immediately ordered two battleships, the "London" and the "Prince of Wales," to reinforce the fleet in addition to the "Queen" and "Implacable."

On the same day the War Council authorised "the First Lord of the Admiralty to inform Vice-Admiral de Robeck that he could continue the naval operations against the Dardanelles if he thought fit."

The War Council did not meet again until the 14th May.

Meanwhile on the 23rd March Admiral de Robeck had met in Council with Generals Hamilton and Birdwood.

Admiral de Robeck told us that at this Conference it was apparent to him that an army was necessary to keep his lines of communication and that to effect this it was "necessary to hold the Peninsula."

While ready to continue the action he therefore telegraphed that day to the Admiralty his opinion that "a decisive operation about the middle of next month appears to me better than to take great risks for what may well be only half measures."

The final decision to abandon the naval attack was told by Mr. Churchill in his statement to us in the following words:—

"We discussed the whole question at length on the morning of the 23rd at our daily meeting (*i.e.*, of the War Group at the Admiralty), Sir Henry Jackson being present.

I proposed that we should direct the Admiral to renew the naval attack according to his previous intention. The First Sea Lord, however, did not agree; nor did Sir A. Wilson. Nor did Sir Henry Jackson. Lord Fisher took the line that hitherto he had been willing to carry the enterprise forward, because it was supported and recommended by the Commander on the spot. But now that Admiral de Robeck and Sir Ian Hamilton had decided upon a joint operation, we were bound to accept their view. I do not at all blame Lord Fisher for this decision. The arguments for it were very strong indeed.

Both the Prime Minister and Mr. Balfour, with whom I discussed the matter, were inclined to my view, but as our professional advisers and the Admiral on the spot were against it, it was impossible to go further, and I bowed to their decision, but with regret and anxiety."

The naval attack on the Narrows was never resumed.

The story of the landing on the 25th April, the preparations which preceded it, the delay in concentrating troops for the subsequent operations, do not come within the scope of this memorandum.

I wish to record the following conclusions:—

(1) The facts disclosed in the course of the inquiry show that the War Council concentrated their attention too much on the political ends to be gained by an offensive policy in the East and gave too little attention to the means by which that policy could be translated into terms of naval and military action. The War Council never had before them detailed staff estimates of men, munitions, and material, or definite plans showing them what military operations were possible.

The War Council also underestimated without any real investigation the strength of the Turkish opposition.

(2) The War Council rejected without sufficient consideration all previous opinions against a purely naval attack on forts. The problem of forcing the Dardanelles, even by a purely naval attack, required the consideration of the expert engineer and artilleryman as much as that of the expert naval officer, and should therefore have been submitted to a joint naval and military staff for investigation.

(3) Mr. Churchill failed to present fully to the War Council the opinions of his naval advisers, and this failure was due to his own strong personal opinion in favour of a naval attack. Mr. Churchill should also have consulted the Board of Admiralty before such a large and novel departure in naval policy was undertaken.

(4) It is difficult to understand why the War Council did not meet between the 19th March and the 14th May. The failure of the naval attack on the 18th March showed the necessity of abandoning the plan of forcing the passage of the Dardanelles by purely naval operations. The War Council should then have met and considered fully the future policy to be pursued.

(5) Important political advantages were gained by the first success of the naval attack and the possibility of further success. But these advantages would not have continued unless further operations had been undertaken at the Dardanelles or elsewhere in the East after the failure of the naval attack on the 18th March.

(6) Finally, I strongly recommend that operations of a similar character should in future be thoroughly considered by a joint naval and military staff before they are undertaken. It is essential for the success of such operations that both the Navy and the Army should be recognized as integral factors consulting and co-operating in the common policy to be pursued.

WALTER ROCH

In its second report, which will also be published in this series, the Dardanelles Commission analysed the disastrous military and naval campaign which followed.

It has been estimated that some 400,000 troops were deployed in this campaign on the side of the Allies, and that their losses amounted to some 252,000. Turkish losses were estimated at 251,000.

Other titles in the series

John Profumo and Christine Keeler, 1963

"The story must start with Stephen Ward, aged fifty. The son of a clergyman, by profession he was an osteopath ... his skill was very considerable and he included among his patients many well-known people ... Yet at the same time he was utterly immoral."

The Backdrop
The beginning of the '60s saw the publication of 'Lady Chatterley's Lover' and the dawn of sexual and social liberation as traditional morals began to be questioned and in some instances swept away.

The Book
In spite of the recent spate of political falls from grace, the Profumo Affair remains the biggest scandal ever to hit British politics. The Minister of War was found to be having an affair with a call girl who had associations with a Russian naval officer at the height of the Cold War. There are questions of cover-up, lies told to Parliament, bribery and stories sold to the newspapers. Lord Denning's superbly written report into the scandal describes with astonishment and fascinated revulsion the extraordinary sexual behaviour of the ruling classes. Orgies, naked bathing, sado–masochistic gatherings of the great and good and ministers and judges cavorting in masks are all uncovered.

ISBN 0 11 702402 3   Price £6.99

War 1914:Punishing the Serbs

" ... I said that this would make it easier for others such as Russia to counsel moderation in Belgrade. In fact, the more Austria could keep her demand within reasonable limits, and the stronger the justification she could produce for making any demands, the more chance there would be for smoothing things over. I hated the idea of a war between any of the Great Powers, and that any of them should be dragged into a war by Serbia would be detestable."

The Backdrop
In Europe before WWI, diplomacy between the Embassies was practised with a considered restraint and politeness which provided an ironic contrast to the momentous events transforming Europe forever.

The Book
Dealing with the fortnight leading up to the outbreak of the First World War, the book mirrors recent events in Serbia to an astonishing extent. Some argued for immediate and decisive military action to punish Serbia for the murder of the Archduke Franz Ferdinand. Others pleaded that a war should not be fought over Serbia. The powers involved are by turn angry, conciliatory and, finally, warlike. Events take their course as the great war machine grinds into action.

ISBN 0 11 702410 4   Price £6.99

The British Invasion of Tibet:
Colonel Younghusband, 1904

"On the 13th January I paid ceremonial visit to the Tibetans at Guru, six miles further down the valley in order that by informal discussion I might assure myself of their real attitude. There were present at the interview three monks and one general from Lhasa. These monks were low-bred persons, insolent, rude and intensely hostile; the generals, on the other hand, were polite and well-bred."

The Backdrop

At the turn of the century, the British Empire was at its height, with its army at the forefront of the mission to bring what the Empire saw as the tremendous civilising benefits of the British way of life to those nations which it regarded as still languishing in the dark ages.

The Book

In 1901, a British missionary force under the leadership of Colonel Francis Younghusband crossed over the border from British India and invaded Tibet. Younghusband insisted on the presence of the Dalai Lama at meetings to give tribute to the British and their Empire. The Dalai Lama merely replied that he must withdraw. Unable to tolerate such an insolent attitude, Younghusband marched forward and inflicted considerable defeats on the Tibetans in several one-sided battles.

ISBN 0 11 702409 0   Price £6.99